The Scarecrow Author Bibliographies

Scarecrow Author Bibliographies, No. 43

LIBRARY
BRYAN COLLEGE
DAYTON, TN. 37321

Christopher Marlowe

An annotated bibliography of criticism since 1950

Kenneth Friedenreich

Foreword by
Richard Levin

The Scarecrow Press, Inc.
Metuchen, N.J., & London   1979

68881

Library of Congress Cataloging in Publication Data

Friedenreich, Kenneth, 1947-
  Christopher Marlowe, an annotated bibliography of
criticism since 1950.

  (The Scarecrow author bibliographies ; no. 43)
  Includes indexes.
  1. Marlowe, Christopher, 1564-1593--Bibliography.
I. Title.
Z8550.4.F75 [PR2674]   016.822'3   79-17646
ISBN 0-8108-1239-8

Copyright © 1979 by Kenneth Friedenreich
Manufactured in the United States of America

FOR MY PARENTS

and

To the Memory of Irving Ribner,

Marlowe Scholar, Teacher, Friend

CONTENTS

FOREWORD

I was happy to accept Kenneth Friedenreich's kind invitation
to contribute a Foreword to this volume, because I believe that
the type of study he has undertaken here responds to a very real
and pressing need in the ongoing enterprise of literary scholarship. The current state of that enterprise in the field of
English Renaissance drama, and indeed in most other fields, presents us with an unsettling paradox, for it is undoubtedly much
more vigorous and exciting now than in any earlier period, and at
the same time seems to be more confused and uncertain. Over
the past few decades we have been seeing an extraordinary increase in both the number and the variety of investigations directed toward the enhancement of our understanding and ap-
preciation of that drama; but this apparent gain has been largely
offset by a corresponding increase in the amount and intensity of
disagreement to be found in the results of these investigations.
And this phenomenon is perhaps nowhere more evident than in
the recent work on Christopher Marlowe.

It is not equally true, to be sure, of all areas of Marlowe
scholarship. In the study of his life, his sources and intellectual
background, his language, his text, and his theater, there has
been some progressive expansion of our knowledge, where it has
been possible for later research to build upon the achievements of
the past, as Mr. Friedenreich's comments in the following pages
will show (although they will also show that this progress has
been far from steady, and is still troubled by a number of basic
controversies). But in the interpretation of the plays themselves,
which presumably is the ultimate purpose of those studies of his
life and sources and background and language and text and theater, no such progress is discernible. I think it would be fair to say
(and this too can be verified by the commentary in the bibliography) that we do not now have anything even approaching a con-
sensus on the meaning or the intended effect of any of his major

works. Instead we encounter the widest variety of conflicting—
and sometimes flatly contradictory—interpretations, for in this
area the practitioners all too typically proceed, not by building
upon the labors of their predecessors, but by rejecting them, in
order to propound yet another "new reading" whose claim to our
attention rests upon the assertion that it has never been thought
of before. It is certainly possible, as Mr. Friedenreich points out,
to trace definite trends or fashions in these new readings, but
there is no reason to believe that the latest trends bring us any
closer to Marlowe's intention than those which they have temporarily replaced.

We may well ask, then, what can be done about this state of
affairs? One could, of course, simply decide to do nothing—to
accept what appears to be the prevailing attitude of laissez-faire,
in which each entrepreneur minds his own business of producing
new readings and expects his competitors to do the same. But if
we believe that the interpretation of literature really matters, that
it is not merely some pointless game, then it seems to me that we
should try to confront our situation and to improve upon it. And
in such an attempt the bibliographical survey presented in this
volume can be extremely useful, since it outlines for us the evolution and the contours of the current critical scene, the major
areas of controversy which have developed within it, and the
kinds of approaches which have produced them. It gives us,
therefore, the information we must have if we are ever to identify
our problems and to address them directly. And with this information, one might hope, it would be possible to begin some sort
of rational conversation which should clarify these interpretative
problems and so lead us eventually, if not to greater agreement,
then at least to greater insight into the nature of our dis-
agreements, their causes, and their consequences. We would
know just where we now stand, and how we arrived at this point,
and in what directions we can profitably proceed.

Some such stocktaking is needed in any ongoing enterprise
from time to time, in order to digest the work which has been
produced; but in our field the need is now especially urgent, because the amount of material we have been given to digest is so
large and so confusing. If we are to have any chance of making
sense out of it, we must rely upon the kind of broadly assimilative

scholarship represented in this bibliography and other similar undertakings. They may not seem as glamorous as the creation of another new reading of *Doctor Faustus,* but they are likely to be of more lasting value.

RICHARD LEVIN

State University of New York at Stony Brook

PREFACE

Perusing brief annotations cannot take the place of reading through works about Marlowe, whether they are notes or lengthy books. However, users of this bibliography will be in a better position to determine which materials to pursue further. The abundant annual harvest in Marlowe studies in particular and Renaissance literature in general has meant a proliferation of publications that both libraries and individuals have had difficulty in keeping up with. In some cases the entries below will of necessity be as close to certain items as students of the subject come. Dissertations, save in a few instances, are not annotated because most libraries possess back numbers of *Dissertation Abstracts International*, from which students can learn the scope and methods of particular doctoral theses.

Annotations take a variety of forms depending on the items. Notes are boiled down from their already terse dimensions to one or two seminal points or salient details. Some journal articles and essays in books are paraphrased in several sentences. For instance, a paper claiming that *Doctor Faustus* is an inverted saint's life does not require much more detail than pointing out its effect on the work. Students curious to find out the specifics of this essay will need to locate the full article. In others, direct quotation best represents the author's purposes. Still others combine paraphrase and direct quotation. Annotations for books are usually set out in greater detail, and reviews are also indicated for important or controversial studies. Where works are of particular notoriety, interest, or value, I do not hesitate to say so, though the seasoned scholar will probably detect my prejudice that Marlowe was a better dramatist than received critical opinion has usually allowed.

This work is intended to centralize conveniently the listings and abstracts provided by the *MLA Annual Bibliography* published by the Modern Language Association, *The Annual Bibliography of English Literature* published by the Modern Humanities Research Association, and *Abstracts of English Studies* published by the National Council of Teachers of English. That this last publication has fallen well behind the current calendar year in its brave work is only additional testimony to the mountains of criticism produced annually in English and American literature. I do not pretend to offer an exhaustive listing, only a thorough one. Certain obscure foreign-language items are omitted, as are some items which deal only in passing with Marlowe and then repeat generally accepted opinion. Where editorial principles in Section 1 seem important to mention, I do so, but do not as a general rule. While I take full responsibility for these decisions, I feel the work can be of service and interest to specialist and general reader alike.

The year 1950 seems appropriate as a beginning for this work as it marks the publication of W. W. Greg's fascinating edition of the parallel texts of *Doctor Faustus (30)*. His work in many respects seems to incorporate so much of what was learned by Greg himself, and by other pioneers in bibliography and textual criticism during the first half of the twentieth century—McKerrow, Pollard, Chambers, Dover Wilson, to name but a few. They have made the Marlowe canon more accessible by their labors.

Within a few years, too, of our *terminus a quo*, Marlowe criticism underwent a shift. The predominant "romantic" school of interpretation which saw his heroes as spokesmen for Marlowe's own unorthodox views was challenged successfully (though not supplanted) by a more "modern" or "ironic" school of criticism. This line of interpretation sees Marlowe as objective and detached artist, intensely critical of his protagonists and ambiguous in his perception of the worlds they imagine or fashion for themselves. The essay following is intended to assess the considerable value of the earlier criticism and to suggest also what avenues future Marlowe studies might investigate.

By way of acknowledgment, I wish to thank numerous librarians who cheerfully answered my queries at the Perry Y. Casteñada Library at The University of Texas at Austin and at Trinity University in San Antonio.

I am grateful to Dr. Michael F. Kelly, Director of the
John Peace Memorial Library at The University of Texas at San
Antonio, for his assistance. I also wish to thank those colleagues
around the country who responded to my call in *PMLA* (May
1977) for papers and offprints. I also thank *PMLA* for the space.
Professor Clifford C. Huffman, friend and one-time colleague,
allowed me to peruse the relevant pages of his revised *Tudor and
Stuart Drama Bibliography*. My friend and mentor, Professor
Richard Levin, of the State University of New York at Stony
Brook, has given me much guidance and valuable instruction by
the example of his own fine work in Renaissance Drama, and I
am happy that he has provided a perceptive foreword for this
work. My colleague, Professor Gary Lane, who encouraged me to
do this project initially, also has my deep thanks, as does Professor Peter Morrison for his cogent criticisms of my introductory
essay. My wife Donna has patiently endured my mutterings about
progress on this work and has been delightfully supportive. While
my dedication speaks for itself, I regret that Professor Ribner is
no longer contributing his wit and judgment to the issues current
in Marlowe criticism. We who had the good fortune of studying
with Irving during his final years at Stony Brook learned much
from him.

September, 1978
Laguna Beach, CA

MARLOWE CRITICISM AND *ON THE ORIGIN OF SPECIES*[1]

In two previous papers I made passing reference to the biographical and idolatrous approach to Marlowe's life and works that modern criticism inherited from the late nineteenth century.[2] The present occasion seems to merit a closer look at some representative Victorian critics of Marlowe in order to assess the general course of opinion from their day until 1950, the starting point of this bibliography. In his book on medieval drama, O. B. Hardison, Jr. observes that "At the end of *The Origin of Species* (1859), Darwin called for an evolutionary treatment of subjects relating to man. Within the next twenty years Darwinian concepts became pervasive in studies of culture, including literary scholarship" (4). We need not go very far to find evidence that supports Hardison's claim. Writing about Shakespeare's predecessors in 1883, John Addington Symonds declares that "The style of England, the expression of our race in a specific form of art, grew steadily, instinctively, spontaneously, by evolution from within" (4). The basic trend in the historically oriented study of Shakespeare and his contemporaries from the mid-nineteenth century onwards is on *progress*, material and measurable, from an earlier primitive drama. Drama was considered the culmination of the Renaissance in England, the crown of its achievement. Shakespeare was its richest jewel, set off even from other precious stones like Marlowe and Jonson. While Hardison and others in recent years have provided a necessary corrective for the evolutionary bias in the criticism of medieval drama, the task remains to be done for Shakespeare and his contemporaries, particularly Christopher Marlowe.

Marlowe, like his contemporaries, was a beneficiary of Victorian industriousness. Alexander Dyce in 1850 completed the first of his two editions of Marlowe's works; the second appeared in 1858. After Dyce came A. H. Bullen's edition in 1885. Along with the Reverend Alexander B. Grosart, Bullen deserves credit for providing modern editions of many Renaissance writers whose work had not in many cases been reprinted since the sixteenth and seventeenth centuries. Two years after Bullen's edition, in 1887, Havelock Ellis provided through the Mermaid Drama Series an inexpensive text of Marlowe's plays for the general reader.

At the center, of course, of all such industry was Shakespeare himself. Between 1850 and 1900 his works were published in fifteen different, important editions, including the well-known Globe text (1864). Though the Shakespeare Society ceased to function in 1853, the New Shakespeare Society flourished between 1874 and 1894. Numerous critical studies were published too, of which perhaps Edward Dowden's *Shakspere, A Critical Study of His Mind and Art* (1875) and his *Shakspere Primer* (1877) are the foremost expressions of their time on the subject. Dowden sought to integrate the known facts of Shakespeare's life with a conception of a man possessing a deepening intellect, spirituality, and mastery of dramatic form and expression. The Darwinian model fits Dowden's Shakespeare: he evolves. In the *Primer,* Dowden traces this evolution by stages. Shakespeare's early career is called "In the Workshop," while the period of the great comedies following is called "In the World." The sequence of great tragedies commencing with *Hamlet* finds Shakespeare moving "Out of the Depths" and "On to the Heights" in the final plays. Out of the suffering—implicitly the romantic pre-condition necessary for great art—which produced the tragedies, the Shakespeare of the last plays is a demigod, according to Dowden. The mystery and mastery of art are awesomely embodied in Shakespeare's alter ego, the magician Prospero. Dowden's interpretation of Shakespeare's career, his outer theatrical life and his interior spiritual existence, is really a panegyric to genius marked by continual activity and guided by discipline: "There can be no doubt that Shakspere considered it worth his while to be prudent, industrious, and economical . . . he made himself useful in every possible way to his dramatic company. While others, Greene, and Peele, and Marlowe, had squandered their strength in the turbulent life on London, Shakspere husbanded his strength" (31–32). Dowden's great critical study still deservedly remains in print; from our vantage, furthermore, we see that

Dowden saw Shakespeare's triumph not only in terms of art, but also in terms of the Victorian love of hard work and the Darwinian belief that only the fittest survive.

We can see already from Dowden that the part played by Christopher Marlowe in this pageant of evolution is quite another matter. His poetic genius, celebrated in the Renaissance by Jonson and Drayton and many others, was never questioned by posterity. However, his life and character, as these were excoriated by Puritans from almost the time of his death in 1593, suggested that Marlowe was a genius of a different sort than Shakespeare. He thunders onto the scene with *Tamburlaine* and follows his huge success with a series of other characters writ large, who leave auditors astonished, outraged, confused, and amused: Faustus, Barabas, the Guise, Edward II, Mortimer. No workshops for Marlowe. He stains the drama of time past, and lights the time to come. What his works promise for the stage, Shakespeare's works fulfill immeasurably. The facts of his short and violent life make Marlowe the perfect foil for the other man who, though not an Oxbridge product, possesses more comprehensive knowledge of man. Needless to say, critics have never tired of comparing the two men, frequently in the invidious terms that Dowden uses to cast Marlowe as the lesser of them.

Marlowe was seen to embody the Dionysian and Byronic energies of "the Artist" which Shakespeare could appreciate but keep under his control. It is hardly a wonder, then, that by the close of the nineteenth century Marlowe was frequently viewed as a romantic out of place among the less flamboyant, more sober intelligences of the Elizabethan era. He was, in the evolution of drama, either the first primate or the last ape, depending on one's perspective. He seemed to have been carried off prematurely so that the greater genius of Shakespeare might have room enough to bustle in. The career of "Kit Marlowe" was suited to the Victorian impression of progress in the drama; their conceptions of the man and artist hardened into critical commonplaces—one reason, surely, that subsequent commentary moves to and from extremes. How else, for instance, can we read one critic claiming that Marlowe's *Doctor Faustus* is godless and bleak, while another insists that the play affirms Christianity?

The critical commonplaces inherited from the Victorians about Marlowe are numerous; all reflect the evolutionary bias in interpretation of the drama and the dramatist, implicitly or explicitly. The following passages best represent them:

1.   Shakspere saw one thing clearly, that if the time ever came when he would write tragedy, the tragedy must be of a kind altogether different from that created upon Marlowe's method,—the method of idealising passions on a gigantic scale. To add to the pieces of the school of Marlowe a rhapsody of blood commingled with nonsense was impossible for Shakspere, who was never altogether wanting in sane judgment, and a lively sense of the absurd.   [Dowden, p. 98]

2.   In dealing with Marlowe, it is impossible to separate the poet from the dramatist, the man from his creations. His personality does not retire, like Shakespeare's, behind the work of art into impenetrable mystery. Rather, like Byron, but with a truer faculty for dramatic presentation than Byron possessed, he inspires the principal characters of his tragedies with the ardour, the ambition, the audacity of his own restless genius.   [Symonds, p. 498]

3.   [Marlowe's] characters are not so much human beings, with the complexity of human attributes combined in living personality, as types of humanity, the animated moulds of human lusts and passions which include, each one of them, the possibility of many individuals. . . . This tendency to dramatise ideal conceptions, to vitalize character with one dominant and tyrannous motive, is very strong in Marlowe.   [Symonds, pp. 484–485]

4.   Marlowe showed stupendous power in exciting terror and pity; but it is in single situations rather than in clear-eyed development of the plot that his power is seen at its highest. Shakespeare's sympathy with humanity in all its phases was infinite; Marlowe was a lofty egoist, little moved by the joys and sorrows of ordinary mortals. The gift of radiant humour, which earned Shakespeare the title of gentle among his contemporaries, was denied to Marlowe.   [Bullen, I, lxxiii]

5. Marlowe has little or no humour. [*Ibid.*, lxxvi]

6. [Marlowe was] the young poet who swept from the English stage the tatters of barbarism, and habited Tragedy in stately robes; who was the first to conceive largely, and exhibit souls struggling in the Bonds of circumstance.
[*Ibid.*, lxxxiv]

7. It seems likely that the last years of Marlowe's life grew careless and irregular; his later plays (putting aside *Edward II*) show signs of swift and over-hasty workmanship. . . . At the same time the thirst after the infinite and impossible dies out, and is replaced by no sane and cheerful content with earth's limits. . . . Marlowe, like Cyril Tourneur, lacked altogether the tender humanity, the sweet and genial humour which saved the sensitive Shakespeare from the bitter pride of genius. . . . Marlowe was always outspoken, one gathers, and at this time it appears that he attracted especial attention as a freethinker. . . . It is noteworthy that Marlowe's heroes are usually heathens or infidels, and he takes every opportunity of insinuating a sceptical opinion. [Ellis, p. xxix]

8. He first, and he alone, guided Shakespeare into the right way of work; . . . he is the greatest discoverer, the most daring and inspired pioneer, in all our literature. Before him there was neither genuine blank verse nor a genuine tragedy in our language. After his arrival the way was prepared, the paths were made straight, for Shakespeare.
[Swinburne, p. 14]

These eminent Victorian and Edwardian critics give Marlowe his due as a poetic genius. Indeed, Symonds' pages about Marlowe's dramatic verse strike me as still some of the most perceptive and intelligent assessments of it. In maintaining their evolutionary bias towards the literature, the critics credit Marlowe with making the transition from "barbarism" to dignity in drama, implying as well that without him, Shakespeare's accomplishment might have suffered. All of this is high praise. On the other hand, however, in their unwillingness to separate the scurrilous suppositions about Marlowe the man from their evaluations of his creative faculties, these same commentators, almost in unanimity, made assumptions that have vexed us since. These are 1) that Marlowe wrote about passions rather than people; 2) that his plays frequently degenerate into nonsense or excess; 3) perhaps most important, that his characters invariably mouth his own held opinions; 4) that his characters were mere puppets, vessels containing his ideals and opinions so that, 5) Marlowe lacks sympathy or compassion for ordinary people; 6) he has no sense of humor; 7) he cannot fully realize a plot and is disinterested in dramatic structure; 8) he is a great poet but not a great playwright. These commonplaces stem directly or indirectly from comparisons between Marlowe and Shakespeare, and beyond them, as expressed by Dowden and by Ellis, is an implication that something about Marlowe's work is abnormal and even insane. Such an opinion can only be reconciled with the contrary praise of Marlowe as a pioneer if critics were willing to imagine that Marlowe himself was as bad as his first Puritan detractors made him out to be—on to which conception no small degree of Byronic stereotypes had been grafted. Marlowe was both a "serious artist" and a precocious bad boy who lived too hard and died too young. University wit, savant, poet, spy, alleged homosexual, brawler, fifth columnist, keeper of dubious companions. We have had to contend with these commonplaces because our forebears argued their opinions with so much forcefulness and self-assurance, and because it has been impossible to deny what they stated in terms of evolution—Marlowe is the pivotal figure of transition between Shakespeare and the earlier drama.

The commonplaces inherited from the Victorian and Edwardian critics of Marlowe have affected subsequent commentary in a variety of ways. First was the Marlowe Canon. If it was assumed that Marlowe had no sense of humor, then it could also be assumed that the comic elements of his plays were written by other, lesser men. Because Marlowe's heroes embodied great ideas, they could not also be pranksters and jokers. The temptation to disintegrate the canon was very strong. In his important single-volume, old-spelling edition of *The Works* (1911), Tucker Brooke printed the 1604 (A-text), of *Doctor Faustus* as best representing the author's original intentions; the 1616 (B-text), generally accepted today, was relegated to an appendix. Similarly, this editor terms the changes between the first and latter portions of *The Jew of Malta* as a decline from "vigorous flow of tragic

interest and character portrayal [into] . . . a wilderness of melodrama and farce" (232). And although, as early as 1919, T. S.
Eliot suggested that Marlowe's *Jew* was a "tragic farce," his opinion was ignored for many decades after.[3]

The period between Tucker Brooke's edition and the end of
World War II saw significant advances in Marlowe biography,
too, though it soon becomes clear that new evidence reinforced
the commonplaces inherited from the Victorians. In 1925, Leslie
Hotson uncovered in the Public Records Office the testimony of
the Coroner's Inquest that exonerated Ingram Frizer from responsibility for Marlowe's death. The evidence suggests that a
cantankerous Marlowe brought about his own violent death and,
despite a legion of others crying "Conspiracy," beginning with
Dr. Samuel A. Tannenbaum (1928), Hotson's discovery has generally been accepted. Thanks to Hotson, it appears, the precocious bad boy image of Marlowe is confirmed, even enriched by
others.

In *Christopher Marlowe and His Circle* (1929), F. S. Boas
knows that our natural sympathies will always be with Marlowe
because he "comes trailing the clouds of glory of the pioneer, of
the herald of the dramatic day" (135). But he concludes in light of
Hotson's discovery that "the fact remains that the evidence from
various sources is consistent, and . . . presents a figure of passionate and restless intellect, quick at word and blow, equally
ready with the dagger-point and the no less piercing edge of a
ruthless dialectic" (136–137). Two years later, in 1931, J. M.
Robertson's *Marlowe: A Conspectus* reviews the evidence and
speculates that Marlowe's legal troubles in the last weeks of his
life may have been instigated by Thomas Kyd out of jealousy,
because "It was Marlowe who had chiefly eclipsed him on the
stage" (27). But Robertson largely endorses Hotson's evidence
and molds it to suit his conception of Marlowe the man: "if we
are to think of him aright, we must conceive the genially reckless
man of genius who was so far a natural dramatist that the sangui-
nary spectacle of Renaissance life struck him as a fitting theme for
poetry"; Robertson adds that because Marlowe "lacked alike
humour and native tenderness . . . his poetry, in which he seeks
and finds his final distinction, is essentially descriptive rather than
dramatic" (55–56; 60).

Then, in 1937, Philip Henderson in *And Morning in His Eyes* (pp. 199–200) endorses Hotson and goes on to expand on how Marlowe's violent death is a reflection of his work and character. Henderson believes that Marlowe was by nature "frustrated"—"We see it in the violent rebellious quality of his work, and in its fragmentariness. After all allowances have been made for corrupt texts and interpolations, the fact remains that he never achieved in any of his works the harmonious completion of a Spenser or a Shakespeare" (330). Further, "Marlowe's approach to his subject was always intensely personal and introspective, in contrast to Shakespeare's great objectivity. . . . each of his heroes is seldom more than the embodiment of his own frustrated desires."

Three other major works of scholarship published before 1950 reiterate the commonplaces as well. First is F. S. Boas' *Christopher Marlowe: A Biographical and Critical Study* (1940), still highly regarded today. Having weighed the evidence, he surmises that Marlowe's "life record forms a drama as absorbing as any of his own tragedies" (308) and finds the deficiencies of his dramatic technique compensated for by the force of personality:

> It was part of technique to capture at once the eyes and ears of the theatre audience with an arresting opening and to send them home at the close enthralled by an elaborately worked up *finale*. In the intervening scenes he paid relatively little attention to the articulation of the plot. . . . He had not the prodigal creative faculty that is the supreme attribute of the world's master-dramatists, though the minor figures in his plays are often firmly enough outlined within a brief compass. His distinctive achievement was to endow the protagonists in his dramas with his own elemental vitality. (312)

The second work is John Bakeless' two-volume *The Tragicall History of Christopher Marlowe* (1942), which intended to "bring together everything that can now be known about Christopher Marlowe" (vii). The study is so copious that while it has never replaced Boas as the standard biographical record, it remains valuable in bringing together so much information. Bakeless says that the mass of evidence as to Marlowe's unorthodoxy is no doubt rather confused and sometimes contradictory, but that it is possible to elicit from it pretty clear general ideas of Marlowe's religious beliefs. Plainly he is not an orthodox and unquestioning Protestant. . . . [His] religious views were subject to cold philosophical scrutiny which, to the average mind of that day or this, would have seemed flatly atheistic. . . . Marlowe is the least adept of dramatists in concealing himself. (I, 139–140)

For Bakeless, Marlowe worked without models; he says (unconsciously paraphrasing Swinburne) that Marlowe "was making straight the path . . . for a greater genius than himself" (II, 3).

The final study appeared in 1946, Paul H. Kocher's *Christopher Marlowe: A Study of His Thought, Learning, and Character.* He announces straightaway that Marlowe was a "subjective artist" (3) and goes on to demonstrate from the mass of evidence, which Bakeless had termed "rather confused and sometimes contradictory," a consistent portrait of Marlowe as a deep thinker and religious skeptic. Kocher stresses unduly the importance of Baines' allegations against Marlowe; nonetheless he does break with the past in supposing that Marlowe was a bitter humorist, and one suspects that Kocher is basically correct in noting that the emphasis in the plays shifts from a celebration of power for its own sake to an understanding that compassion is the true measure of human value.

Along with these heavily documented works, the major critical study of Marlowe during this period was written in 1927 by Una M. Ellis-Fermor. Her study attempts to do for Marlowe what Dowden had done for Shakespeare fifty years before. Ellis-Fermor maintains that Marlowe's plays cannot finally stand up to the weight of their creator's thought. The plays are vehicles for Marlowe's own ideas and frustrations, as illustrated by her comment that *Doctor Faustus* reflects that Marlowe's own mind "had been denied the things needful to its development and had been forced to submit itself to years of fruitless and unproductive effort" (89–90). Unlike Shakespeare, she concludes,

Christopher Marlowe does not traffic in the affairs of men, nor does he record or illuminate the everyday world. . . . For

man's relation to man he cared by nature hardly at all; man's
relation to God and to the universe was his whole creation. . . . The Elizabethan world is never photographed or
portrayed in his works; but its ideas and aspirations find
nowhere truer revelation; none of his contemporaries reflect
its spirit, its desire and efforts better than he. (132–140,
passim)

Fundamentally, the first modern scholars, biographers, and
critics of Marlowe *as a dramatist* broke no new ground, offered
no new insights, and rarely questioned the critical commonplaces
they inherited from the nineteenth-century writers. Each in the
last analysis subordinates Marlowe's work to a consideration of
Marlowe the man. Each is unwilling to grant Marlowe the talent
of "negative capability" which Shakespeare possessed abundantly.
Each is unwilling to allow that Marlowe could invent a character
or situation without thrusting himself into either. Each celebrates
his genius by enumerating the defects of his plays—a peculiarity
when each also claims that his dramas made the way "straight" for
Shakespeare. These are not apparent discrepancies but serious
contradictions: Marlowe himself cannot be "a great artist" if his
"art" is rude or inferior; he could not have made an impact in the
theater of his day unless he understood its potential and exploited
it as a playwright, not as an atheist, not as the mirror of "ideas" of
the "Elizabethan world" or "Renaissance skepticism" or some
other convenient historical construct.

The study of the life and works of Marlowe exhibits simultaneously some the best and many of the worst qualities of historical criticism, of literary biography, and of creating a sense of the
past. Compared to many of his contemporaries, we possess today
a wealth of knowledge about Marlowe's life and a detailed account
of his death. Paradoxically, this knowledge has not often been
profitably applied. We have record of contemporary estimations
by poets and dramatists and by polemicists, time-servers, and
spies. Consider, for the moment, the horrendous account of Marlowe's death in Thomas Beard's *Theatre of Gods Judgements*
(1597), a work reprinted many times thereafter into the mid-
seventeenth century. The death is an exemplum, a warning to
those who, like Marlowe, "denied God and his sonne Christ, and

not only in word blasphemed the trinitie, but also . . . wrote bookes against it" (*cf.* Bakeless, I, 144). Beard is intensely partisan, of course, and all but the most naive would misconstrue his view of Marlowe as Puritan propaganda. It is extreme. Nonetheless, the scurrilous allegations against Marlowe by parties with obvious or hidden axes to grind have been used in modern scholarship and inquiry as "evidence" in the academic sense of the word, abundantly supported in footnotes. Yet would we, in our own time, take as "evidence" of Brecht's character a denunciation penned by a Nazi propagandist? Would we, at present, take at face value the estimate of Alexander Solzhenitsyn's personal opinions written by a reviewer in the current Soviet press? The answer to both questions is obvious.

In their penetrating study of literary criticism, William K. Wimsatt and Cleanth Brooks point out that by the close of the nineteenth century two apparently contrary approaches to writers and their works coalesced: "the force of hardheaded, sceptical, factfinding, textual, bibliographical and biographical antiquarianism, and both augmenting this force and being augmented by it, the force of devotion to poetic genius, to the personality, originality, mind and emotion, virtues and vices, life, suffering, and death of the literary creator. The concept of life and sufferings included all kinds of influences upon the creator, and hence no contradiction had to arise between personal study and more deterministic conceptions of national history, sociology, or politics."[4] The rationale for such a harmony came from H. A. Taine and F. Brunetière—the nineteenth-century French critics who argued for the evolutionary bias in the study of literature.[5] Marlowe's "life and sufferings" clearly were as attractive as, if not more so than, the study of his plays and poems. Thus, while the methods of the late Victorian critics seem on the surface not to resemble the more "scholarly" enterprises of major twentieth-century Marlovians before 1950, their conclusions and prejudices and commonplace assumptions are indeed very close.

Challenges of prevailing opinion were few: perusing bibliographies of Marlowe studies published in academic journals during the same period reflects principal interest in Marlowe's comings and goings, and in *Tamburlaine* and *Doctor Faustus*. The other plays are for the most part ignored: for instance, Ribner's 1966 *Tudor and Stuart Drama Bibliography*, partial listing though it is, notes only one study of *Edward II* before 1950. The major endeavor in journal scholarship seems to have been source studies—reflecting the penchant for historicism—designed to "answer" those who believed Marlowe was careless in his approach to writing plays. However, instead of confronting the romantic and subjective approach to Marlowe, these critics (one thinks of Ethel Seaton and Leslie Spence respectively on *Tamburlaine* sources) simply rather glorified Marlowe's "genius" in different way. And, finally, when a modern critic did at last challenge the prevailing conception of Marlowe's character as revealed in his plays, the methodology was basically the same. Roy W. Battenhouse's 1941 study of *Tamburlaine* conceives of the play as a ten-act moral tragedy in which the hero is God's scourge, punishing recalcitrant heathen and Christian alike, destroyed only after he commits the sin of blasphemy. Marlowe, perceived by Battenhouse subjectively behind the scenes, is thus no atheist or skeptic, but rather a persuasive and intelligent Christian. His "evidence" is ingenious and wide-ranging, covering a multitude of historical and moral treatises; it inundates the reader and indeed the plays. Battenhouse deserves our admiration for taking on the Marlowe Establishment and challenging their belief that Marlowe was outrageously unorthodox, though he clearly represents the opposing case in extreme terms. Like them, he offers valuable observations about individual aspects of Marlowe's work, but like them too, he uses the prevailing historical and biographical methods of inquiry to identify the man rather than his plays.

Commentary and criticism since 1950 have continued the debate begun in large measure by Battenhouse, between those who consider Marlowe essentially as a Romantic and subjective artist, and those who follow Battenhouse, if not in conviction, then at least in regarding Marlowe as a more conservative, objective artist whose plays assess Renaissance drives for power, wealth, and knowledge. In either case, Marlowe the dramatist has been ignored until very recently. In the often shrill debates between Marlowe critics, particularly into the early 1960s, many simply refused to address his tangible contributions to dramatic literature, by which I mean something less nebulous than terms such as "tragic dignity" or "idealizing passions." The critical commonplaces inherited from the last century are only now being systematically questioned.

Inevitably, Marlowe's brief career and his accomplishment have suffered in the endless string of comparisons to Shakespeare's career and accomplishment. No one would argue that such inquiries cease, but we must acknowledge that because Marlowe died young, he did not grow as fully as Shakespeare with the practices of the Elizabethan stage. Happily, the work of M. C. Bradbrook, Glynne Wickham, and J. L. Simmons in recent years has shown that Marlowe was sensitive to the potentials and limitations of theatrical conditions. On the other hand, alas (and perhaps its rise was to be expected in view of nearly a century of bad press about the construction and quality of plays), have come a number of books and articles since 1950 which show Marlowe's dramas to be supremely well-made and deviously subtle and clever and ironic. Indeed, the romantic conception of Marlowe in our nuclear age has been replaced by an ironic one that imagines him to be the savage humorist T. S. Eliot long ago said he was. Not surprisingly, the critical method is still one which seeks to find Marlowe himself in his plays.

While the Tamburlaine plays and *Doctor Faustus* have not lacked for attention since 1950, it surprised me to discover that *Edward II* has inspired fewer critics than *Dido, Queen of Carthage*. *The Massacre at Paris* has attracted scant attention: one journal article since 1950. Currently Faustus has come under attack from many who consider him to be a poor scholar; but fortunately the fruitless endeavor of textual disintegration to suit critical prejudices has long fallen into disrepute: Constance B. Kuriyama's recent criticisms of Greg's reconstruction of *Doctor Faustus* seem to indicate a saner trend in canon scholarship. Her task is not to affirm that Marlowe did not write comical scenes because they are comical. Criticism of *Tamburlaine* has fortunately turned away from the "drama of ideas" approach that Ellis-Fermor's study perfected, to problems of its theatrical realization. In studies of the poems, *Hero and Leander* has justly been described as a comic masterpiece, though others would still have us believe that in his Ovidian *tour de force* Marlowe is sneaking some atheism by unsuspecting readers. The recent work of Roma Gill, in particular, with the translations suggests that we have too long ignored Marlowe's techniques and occasional habits in his working with classical texts.

Having liberated ourselves, one hopes, from the misapprehensions of dubious Darwinism and of "lofty egotism" in Marlowe studies, we must look afresh at Marlowe's unique contribution to our culture and literature. We cannot—to paraphrase C. S. Lewis—save the appearances in dealing with the inconsistencies or contradictions concerning his career or canon. Nor should we presume to try, short of discovery of the magnitude of Leslie Hotson's by another young scholar. We have already seen that Hotson's discovery conjured up more ghosts than it laid permanently to rest. Our task remains what it has always been: to respond to some of the most engaging, difficult, paradoxical, and moving drama and poetry written in English—with this caveat offered by David Daiches: "Biography is of little help in evaluating a literary work. . . . Biography may not help us to assess a work, but it is an interesting and illuminating study in its own right. . . . To the serious inquirer of literature, no knowledge comes amiss—but that does not mean that no knowledge is irrelevant to evaluation."[6]

The time is long overdue that we take Christopher Marlowe out of the monkey house.

Notes

1. The title of this essay and its approach, too, are founded on the discussions of the evolutionary bias in medieval drama criticism by O. B. Hardison, Jr., in *Christian Rite and Christian Drama in the Middle Ages* (Baltimore: Johns Hopkins University Press, 1965), especially pp. 1–34. While I am aware, too, that any survey of critical trends is intrinsically historical and thus vulnerable to an "evolutionary bias" of sorts, my central thesis is that in Marlowe's case, while we have perhaps developed more varied approaches, the subjective and autobiographical element assumed in his works still remains an obstacle to evaluation of the plays and poems on their own terms.

To minimize footnote references I include here in order of appearance the works cited in my text. This is not a survey of criticism per se—for fuller accounts of Marlowe's reputation, see Robert Kimbrough (4) and Irving Ribner (199) below. Works here are: John Addington Symonds, *Shakespeare's Predecessors in the English Drama* (London, 1883; rpt. New York, 1966); Edward Dowden, *Shakspere, A Study of His Mind and Art* (1875; London: MacMillan, 1962); A. H. Bullen, ed., *The Works of Christopher Marlowe* (London: John C. Nimmo, 1885); Havelock Ellis, ed., *Christopher Marlowe: Five Plays* (London, 1887; rpt. New York: Hill & Wang, 1956); A. C. Swinburne *The Age of Shakespeare* (London, 1909; rpt. New York: AMS Press, 1967); C. F. Tucker Brooke, ed., *The Works of Christopher Marlowe* (Oxford: Clarendon Press, 1911; rpt. many times after); F. S. Boas, *Christopher Marlowe and His Circle* (London, 1929; rpt. New York: Russell and Russell, 1968); J. M. Robertson, *Marlowe: A Conspectus* (London: George Routledge & Sons, 1931); Philip Henderson, *And Morning in His Eyes* (London: Boriswood, 1937); F. S. Boas, *Christopher Marlowe: A Biographical & Critical Study* (Oxford: Clarendon Press 1940; rev. ed. 1953); John Bakeless, *The Tragicall History of Christopher Marlowe* (1942; rpt. Westport: Connecticut: Greenwood Press, 1970); Paul H. Kocher, *Christopher Marlowe: A Study of His Thought Learning & Character* (Chapel Hill: University of North Carolina Press, 1946); Una M. Ellis-Fermor, *Christopher Marlowe* (London, 1927; rpt. Hamden, Connecticut: Archon, 1967); Roy W. Battenhouse, *Marlowe's Tamburlaine: A Study in Renaissance and Moral Philosophy* (1941; rpt. Vanderbilt University Press, 1964).

2. See "Directions in Tamburlaine Criticism" (529) and "*The Jew of Malta* and the Critics" (471).

3. Related to the matter of the canon was the apocrypha. In 1885, Bullen was certain that *Titus Andronicus*—a work too violent to really belong to Shakespeare—was Marlowe's (lxxvi); *The Taming of a Shrew* could not be Marlowe's because its author "was a genuine humourist" (lxxvi), though subsequent textual studies, beginning with Peter Alexander in 1926 and

John Dover Wilson in 1928, have virtually assured us that no-
body will seriously consider this work Marlowe's. In the late
nineteenth century and the early twentieth century two other
plays were associated with Marlowe, so much in fact that several of the early popular Everyman editions by Edward
Thomas of Marlowe published after the first world war included one of them until 1950. These were *The First Part of
the Contention betwixt the two famous houses of York and
Lancaster* (1594) and *The True Tragedy of Richard Duke of
York* (1595); and it was believed that "Shakespeare worked on
a full and accurate copy of the early plays, and that these early
plays were in large part by Marlowe" (Bullen, p. lxxx), in producing Parts Two and Three of *Henry VI*. Again, in the 1920s
Peter Alexander put the matter to rest as far as Marlowe was
concerned. Additional specious claims of Marlovian authorship
that sprang up in the seventeenth century were dispatched
quickly and Tucker Brooke's edition became our century's first
standard one.

The major authoritative edition to follow Tucker Brooke's
was published between 1930 and 1933 under the general
editorship of R. H. Case, *The Life and Works of Christopher
Marlowe*. Among the subordinate editors were stars of the
Marlowe Establishment—F. S. Boas, Tucker Brooke, Ellis-
Fermor, and H. S. Bennett. Nonetheless, the prevailing critical commonplace that Marlowe possessed no sense of humor
prevented any serious questioning of the A-text of *Doctor
Faustus* or the corruption of *The Jew of Malta*. It was not until
1943 that Leo Kirschbaum argued for the superiority of the
B-text of *Doctor Faustus*, claiming that the 1604 version represents a provincial memorial reconstruction of the play. In his
claim, Kirschbaum anticipates Greg's argument in his parallel
text edition (1950). In 1948 J. C. Maxwell questioned the assumption that *The Jew of Malta* was a bad text, fundamentally
beginning a vindication of the position taken by T. S. Eliot.
Today it is generally assumed that the 1616 text of *Doctor
Faustus* is superior to the earlier one and that *The Jew of
Malta* as we have it represents Marlowe's intentions, despite
discomforts about the broad humor in both plays.

4. William K. Wimsatt and Cleanth Brooks. *Literary Criticism: A
Short History* (New York: Alfred A. Knopf, 1957), p. 533.

5. See Hardison, *op. cit.*, and also Wimsatt and Brooks for discussions of Taine's and Brunetière's contributions to English literary criticism and history, pp. 531–535 and 543–544.

6. David Daiches. *Critical Approaches to Literature* (London: Longmans, 1956), p. 326. For a stimulating, realistic appraisal of the importance of historical knowledge to literary criticism, see E. D. Hirsch, *Validity in Interpretation* (New Haven and London: Yale University Press, 1965), pp. 40ff., and most recently, Ralph Cohen, "Historical Knowledge and Literary Understanding," *PLL*, 14:3 (1978), 227–248; the entire number of *PLL* is devoted to literary and critical theory.

AUTHOR'S NOTE

In an effort to keep the bibliography up-to-date, some twenty-odd entries were added after the manuscript had been edited. These items appear in their appropriate sections and bear an "a" after their entry numbers, a designation that consequently appears in the Index.

1. BIBLIOGRAPHIES, EDITIONS, AND CONCORDANCES

1. Huffman, Clifford Chalmers, comp. "Tudor and Stuart Drama: A Bibliography, 1966–1971." *Educational Theater Journal,* 24 (1972), 169–178.

   A supplement to Irving Ribner, comp., *Tudor and Stuart Drama* (Goldentree Bibliographies). New York: Appleton-Century Crofts, 1966, whose entries run to the year 1965.

2. ———, comp. *Tudor and Stuart Drama.* (Goldentree Bibliographies) O. B. Hardison, Jr., General Editor. Evanston, Illinois: AHM Publishers, 1978.

   An excellent guide for students and scholars alike, bringing together materials in enumerative, largely unannotated fashion. Marlowe entries Nos. 1412–1674.

3. Johnson, Robert C., comp. *Elizabethan Bibliographies Supplements VI: Christopher Marlowe, 1946–1965.* London: Nether Press, 1967.

   Follows up Samuel A. Tannenbaum's *Elizabethan Bibliographies,* itself revised in 1946–47. Entries in the supplement are grouped by years; not annotated.

4. Kimbrough, Robert. "Christopher Marlowe." In *The Predecessors of Shakespeare: A Survey and Bibliography of Recent Studies in English Renaissance Drama.* Terence P. Logan and Denzell S. Smith, eds. Lincoln: University of Nebraska Press, 1973, pp. 3–55.

   A fine survey of the problems of biography, canon, and interpretation about Marlowe, with general assessments of the states of criticism for the respective works. A basic bibliography also included.

5. Palmer, D. J. "Marlowe." In *English Drama excluding Shakespeare: A Select Bibliographical Guide.* Stanley Wells, ed. London: Oxford University Press, 1975, pp. 42–53.

Concise essay surveying the state of scholarship with emphasis on the controversies surrounding Marlowe's alleged atheism, his skepticism, and the relationship of biographical facts to the works. A scant bibliography is provided.

6. Penninger, Frieda Elaine. *English Drama to 1660 (excluding Shakespeare): A Guide to Information Sources.* Detroit: Gale Research Company, 1976. Section 20, "Christopher Marlowe," pp. 285–299.

A useful annotated guide, principally to books about Marlowe published since the late nineteenth century. Provides entries for the Shakespearean authorship claimants on Marlowe's behalf.

6a. Post, Jonathan F. S. "Recent Studies of Marlowe (1968– 1976)." *English Literary Renaissance,* 7 (1977), 382–399.

An excellent overview of the state of criticism in the past several years of considerable activity. Some items, following the format of this series, are briefly annotated or commented upon; others simply listed. Post rightly calls for consideration of Marlowe's abilities as a dramatist, and reiterates Irving Ribner's call (*TDR*, 1964), to examine the impact of classical literature and drama on Marlowe's plays.

7. Ribner, Irving, comp. *Tudor and Stuart Drama.* (Goldentree Bibliographies) New York: Appleton-Century Crofts, 1966. 72 pp.

Marlowe entries, pp. 38–44; supplemented by Huffman, *ETJ,* 24, and revised by Huffman, 1978. (See entry 2.)

EDITIONS

8. Bowers, Fredson, ed. *The Complete Works of Christopher Marlowe.* 2 vols. New York and London: Cambridge University Press, 1973. Vol. I, xi + 417 pp.; Vol. II, 542 pp. Volume I contains *Dido, Tamburlaine, The Jew of Malta,* and *The Massacre at Paris;* Volume II contains *Edward II, Doctor Faustus, The First Book of Lucan, Ovid's Elegies, Hero and Leander,* and Miscellaneous Pieces.

According to the editor, "a critically edited, old-spelling edition of the preserved works of Christoper Marlowe that can be identified with confidence" (p. vii). Brief introductions to each work provide basic summary of bibliographical problems which are detailed in textual notes afterwards. Procedures and copy-text rationale are clearly, if dryly, presented throughout; while the edition makes claim to being the new "standard text," it will only be of real interest to scholars until a volume of commentary and explanatory notes make it useful for the wider audience of readers.

Reviews include a praiseworthy notice in the *Times Literary Supplement* (*TLS* hereafter), 8 February, 1974, p. 130; as well as one expressing some reservation, Lester E. Barber, "A Recent Edition of Marlowe," *Research Opportunities in Renaissance Drama*, 17 (1974), pp. 17–24 (59).

9. Gill, Roma, ed. *The Plays of Christopher Marlowe*. London: Oxford University Press, 1971. 442 pp.

A modern-spelling edition with some explanatory notes intended for the general reader.

10. Kirschbaum, Leo, ed. *The Plays of Christopher Marlowe*. Cleveland and New York: World Publishing Company (Meridian Books), 1962. 495 pp.

Contains five major plays only; *Dido* and *Massacre* are omitted with apologies because "Marlowe's share is not clear" in the former, while the latter's "text is extremely corrupt" (p. 9). The edition proper is a fruition of the editor's textual work—usually on the side of good sense—in the 1940s and early 1950s—and the textual notes make lively reading. There is a glossary at the back of the volume rather than explanatory notes. The edition is most valuable for the lengthy introduction (pp. 10–154), which provides commentary on each scene of each play, in addition to offering stimulating critical judgments: for example, "The Two Machiavellis," "Marlowe and Comedy," and "Religious Values in *Doctor Faustus*."

11. Pendry, E. D. and Maxwell, J. C., eds. *Christopher Marlowe: Complete Plays and Poems*. London: J.M. Dent & Sons, Ltd., and Totowa, New Jersey: Rowman and Littlefield, 1976. xxxix + 543 pp.

A modern-spelling edition of plays and poems; explanatory notes superseded by extensive glossary.

12. Ribner, Irving, ed. *The Complete Plays of Christopher Marlowe.* New York: Odyssey Press, 1963. xl + 432pp.

The aims of the edition are "to make the plays of Marlowe available to the modern student and general reader" (p. ix). Textual notes and select bibliography are concise; the "General Introduction" offers a short biography of Marlowe and also attempts to arrange the plays in an order (culminating with *Dr. Faustus*) that coincides with what the editor believes is Marlowe's development as a dramatist and artist. Pithy explanatory notes throughout the texts of the plays have helped to make this edition an "unofficial" standard one for students, teachers, and many critics.

13. Ridley, M. R., ed. *Christopher Marlowe: Plays and Poems.* (Everyman's Library, No. 383) London: Dent, 1955.

A "portable" edition for the general reader; little critical or textual apparatus. Reviews: Michel Poirier, *Études Anglaises,* 9 (1955), 253; H. Heuer, *Shakesperare Jahrbuch,* 92 (1955), 360.

14. Steane, J. B., ed. *The Complete Plays of Christopher Marlowe.* Harmondsworth and Baltimore: Penguin, 1969. 601 pp.

A student-general reader edition with a fine introduction. Notes and commentary follow text.

The Poems

15. Maclure, Millar, ed. *The Poems: Christopher Marlowe.* (The Revels Edition of the Works of Christopher Marlowe) Clifford Leech, General Editor. London: Methuen & Co., 1968. xliv + 271 pp.

A scholarly edition of the poems, including the Chapman continuation of *Hero and Leander.* Introduction covers in detail the circumstances concerning the composition and publication of the works, as well as providing a brief retrospective of the poems and their early reception (pp. xxxix–xliv). Following the Revels' format, the textual and explanatory notes are printed throughout, below the running text.

16. Orgel, Stephen, ed. *Christopher Marlowe: The Complete Poems and Translations.* (Penguin English Poets Series) Harmondsworth and Baltimore: Penguin, 1971. 283 pp.
A conservative modernization of texts; brief bibliography and no textual notes. Explanatory notes and a Dictionary of Classical names are printed separately after the text. Review: *Times Literary Supplement,* 3 December, 1971, p. 1526.

Hero and Leander

17. Alexander, Nigel. *Elizabethan Narrative Verse.* (Stratford-Upon-Avon Studies, No. 3) Cambridge, Massachusetts: Harvard University Press, 1968. x + 338 pp.
Hero and Leander (both Marlowe and Chapman) in anthology context; uses Blount's 1598A edition as copy text. General historical introduction is a valuable survey of developments in narrative verse from 1560 to 1610. Some notes (pp. 319–325).

18. Donno, Elizabeth Story, ed. *Elizabethan Minor Verse.* New York: Columbia University Press, and London: Routledge & Kegan Paul, 1963; rpt. 1967.
Reproduces *Hero and Leander* (Marlowe and Chapman) with other Elizabethan narratives (pp. 48–126). Slightly modernized old-spelling texts with little or no explanatory or textual apparatus. General introduction is judicious historical survey.

19. *Hero and Leander by Christopher Marlowe: A Facsimile of the First Edition, London, 1598.* With an Introduction and Textual Commentary by Louis L. Martz. Washington, D.C.: Folger Shakespeare Library; New York: Johnson Reprint Corp., 1972.

Ovid's Elegies

20. *Ovids Elegies [tr. by] Christopher Marlowe; Epigrams [of] Sir John Davies, 1595.* Introduction by A. J. Smith. Menston, Yorkshire: Scolar Press, 1973. 162 pp.
A facsimile reprint.

Dido, Queen of Carthage

21. Oliver, H. J., ed. *Dido, Queen of Carthage; The Massacre at Paris.* (The Revels Edition of the Works of Christopher Marlowe) Clifford Leech, General editor. Cambridge, Massachusetts: Harvard University Press; London: Methuen & Co., 1968. lxxvi + 187 pp.

   A scholarly edition of the two plays in the format of this excellent series. Lengthy introduction; extensive explanatory notes and textual notes running beneath the texts.

Edward II

22. Chwat, Jacques, ed. *Edward II.* New York: Bard/Avon Books, 1974. 176 pp.

   A modern-spelling "popular" edition based on the F. N. Lees 1955 revised edition of H. B. Charleton and R. D. Waller's *Edward II,* published in 1933 as one of six volumes in *The Life and Works of Christopher Marlowe* (R. H. Case, General Editor). Includes a brief essay about the play by the editor in addition to printing the "Baines Note" (Appendix I) and Clifford Leech's essay, "Marlowe's *Edward II:* Power and Suffering."

23. Gill, Roma, ed. *Edward II.* With Introduction and Notes. London: Oxford University Press, 1967.

   Modern-spelling edition for the general reader.

24. Merchant, W. Moelwyn, ed. *Edward the Second.* (New Mermaids) New York: Hill & Wang, 1965. xxx + 110 pp.

   Modernized version of 1594 edition published with bibliographical apparatus by W. W. Greg for the Malone Society in 1925. A reasoned introduction argues for Marlowe's mature handling of his subject and historical materials. Textual and explanatory notes run below the text.

25. Ribner, Irving, ed. *Edward II by Christopher Marlowe.* San Francisco: Chandler Publishing Co., 1961.

26. ———, ed. *Edward II: Text and Major Criticism.* New York: Odyssey Press, 1970. ix +213 pp.

Replicated edition and notes of play found in 1963 *Complete Plays*. Reprints three critical essays from journals by Robert Fricker, "The Dramatic Structure of *Edward II*"; Clifford Leech, "Marlowe's *Edward II:* Power and Suffering"; and E. M. Waith, "*Edward II:* The Shadow of Action." Also reprints chapters or relevant sections from books by the following: M. Poirier, Irving Ribner, Wilbur Sanders, David M. Bevington, and Glynne Wickham.

Doctor Faustus

27. Barnet, Sylvan, ed. *Doctor Faustus*. New York: New American Library, 1969.

    A modern-spelling "student" edition featuring a general introduction and explanatory notes running below the text.

28. Bates, Paul A. *Faust: Sources, Works, Criticism*. New York: Harcourt Brace & World, 1969. vii + 218 pp.

    An excellent "student" casebook that includes significant excerpts from the Spies' *Faustbuch* in the modern-spelling version by William Rose (1925; 1963). Reproduces the B-text of *Faustus* based on the editions of F. S. Boas (1932) and Irving Ribner (1963). Also reprints Part I and Act V of Part II of Goethe's *Faust;* Chapter 25 of Thomas Mann's novel *Doctor Faustus* and Karl Shapiro's "Progress of Faust." Reprints three essays dealing with Marlowe's play—Robert Ornstein, "The Comic Synthesis in *Doctor Faustus*," C. L. Barber's "The Form of Faustus' Fortunes Good or Bad," and pages on the play from *English Tragedy before Shakespeare* by Wolfgang Clemen.

29. Gill, Roma, ed. *Doctor Faustus*. (New Mermaids) New York: Hill & Wang, 1965. xxviii + 100 pp.

    Readable and scholarly edition based on the B-text reconstruction by W. W. Greg. Gill maintains the integrity of the text, seeing the comic scenes as "satirical, not farcical; an intelligence is at work, and I suspect it is Marlowe's own" (pp. xviii–xix). Though the play asserts the Christian ethic, "Marlowe's sympathies (if the energy of the verse means anything at all) are for the rebel, the man who is impeded in his pursuit of science, who is frustrated by his efforts to assert his individuality" (xxvii). Textual notes and explanatory notes run below text throughout.

30. Greg, W. W. ed. *Marlowe's Doctor Faustus 1604–1616: Parallel Texts.* Oxford: Clarendon Press, 1950. xiv + 408 pp. Also, W. W. Greg. *The Tragical History of the Life and Death of Doctor Faustus: A Conjectural Reconstruction.* London, New York, Toronto: Oxford University Press, 1950. x + 66 pp.

A monument of applied textual and bibliographical criticism; were his conclusions to be some day overturned (which is not likely), the edition would still remain a model of methodology. Greg's conception of the play and its printed history are elucidated in the "Preface" (pp. vii–viii): "I believe the play to have been originally written by Marlowe in the last year of his life and in collaboration with at least one other playwright, who may have possibly been Samuel Rowley. The text printed in 1604 [A] I believe to represent a reconstruction from memory of the piece as originally performed, but shortened for provincial acting, occasionally interpolated, and progressively adapted to the capacities of a declining company and the taste of a vulgar audience. It preserves, however, almost all Marlowe's share in the composition, and it presents it with substantial fidelity though far from verbal accuracy. The text of 1616 [B] I believe to have been prepared for publication by an editor on the basis of a manuscript containing the authors' drafts from which the prompt-book had in the first instance been transcribed. In the course, however, of preparing the prompt-book, the text underwent an appreciable amount of revision which, of course, found its way into the stage version that underlies the 1604 text. . . . "

Greg's account of the play's composition leads him to the conclusion that Marlowe's share of the play, *Doctor Faustus*, is 825 of 2121 lines. A table (pp. 138–39) summarizes Greg's hypothesis. The conjectural reconstruction, then, is Greg's idea of the play as it was intended for performance.

Numerous reviews of Greg's edition include *TLS* 21 July, 1950, p. 454; M. A. Shaaber, *Modern Language Notes,* 67 (1950), 491–92; J. C. Maxwell, *Cambridge Journal,* 4 (1950), 377–379; Harold Jenkins, *Modern Language Review,* 46 (1950), 82–86; J. M. Nosworthy, *Review of English Studies,* 3 (1950), 68–71; F. C. Danchin, *Letteratura Moderne,* 45 (1950), 267–268; and Fredson

Bowers, *Modern Philology*, 49:2 (1952), 195–204. [For Bowers' review, see 350; also C. B. Kuriyama's "Doctor Greg and *Doctor Faustus*," *English Literary Renaissance*, 5:2 (1975), 171–197.]

31. Jump, John D., ed. *The Tragical History of the Life and Death of Doctor Faustus*. London: Methuen and Co.; Cambridge, Massachusetts: Harvard University Press, 1962. (Revels Edition of the Works of Christopher Marlowe) Clifford Leech, General editor.

    A scholarly one-volume edition of the play that takes very much into account the work of Greg.

32. Kocher, Paul H., ed. *The Tragical History of Doctor Faustus*. 1950.

    A-text (1604) only.

33. Ribner, Irving, ed. *Doctor Faustus: Text & Major Criticism*. New York: Odyssey Press, 1966. viii + 216 pp.

    Text and notes of play replicated from 1963 edition of *Complete Plays;* brief bibliography (pp. 215–216); reprints three articles: Robert Ornstein, "The Comic Synthesis in *Doctor Faustus*"; C. L. Barber's "The Form of Faustus' Fortunes Good or Bad"; and D. J. Palmer, "Language and Magic in *Doctor Faustus*." Relevant chapters or excerpts from books by Una M. Ellis-Fermor (*Christopher Marlowe*, 1927); Harry Levin; Richard B. Sewall; Wolfgang Clemen.

34. Walker, Keith, ed. *Doctor Faustus*. (Fountainwell Drama Texts) Edinburgh: Oliver & Boyd, 1973. 119 pp.

    A reliable old-spelling edition with some notes.

35. Wright, Louis B. and LaMar, Virginia A., eds. *The Tragedy of Doctor Faustus*. New York: Washington Square Press, 1959.

    A bus-stop edition of the A-text in the popularizing manner of Wright's compact Shakespeare editions.

The Jew of Malta.

36. Craik, T. W., ed. *The Jew of Malta*. (New Mermaids) London: Benn; New York: Hill & Wang, 1966. xx + 106 pp.

An excellent edition of play with notes for text and explanations running below. The spelling is modernized, but punctuation largely follows the original. Craik recognizes the worth of the play in terms of the theater: "The play is essentially neither propagandist nor moralistic... but dramatic. Moral questions are not seriously discussed: they are ironically touched upon and left. If moral questions were an important element, the play's interest might be expected to reside as much in the characters as in the plot, but it does not" (p. xiv). The "Introduction" is a fine essay about *The Jew of Malta* as powerful entertainment.

37. Ribner, Irving, ed. *The Jew of Malta: Text and Major Criticism.* New York: Odyssey Press, 1970. xi + 228 pp.
    Reprints text and notes of the 1963 edition of *Complete Plays* with a Selected Bibliography. Reprints J. C. Maxwell's seminal essay, "How Bad Is the Text of *The Jew of Malta?*" as well as Howard S. Babb's "Policy in Marlowe's *The Jew of Malta*"; Alfred Harbage's "Innocent Barabas"; Irving Ribner's "Barabas and Shylock"; G. K. Hunter's "The Theology of Marlowe's *The Jew of Malta*"; and excerpts or relevant chapters from books by F. P. Wilson, M. M. Mahood, J. B. Steane, Douglas Cole, and David M. Bevington.

38. Van Fossen, Richard W., ed. *The Jew of Malta.* (Regents Renaissance Drama Series) Lincoln: University of Nebraska Press; and London: Edward Arnold, 1964. xxx + 122 pp.
    The editor argues that the play's brilliant "theatrical and entertaining design is Marlowe's greatest achievement... but then one remembers that there is also that horrid world of falsity in political, religious, and personal affairs that is perhaps not so grotesquely a distortion of reality as, for the sake of humanity, one might wish" (p. xxv). Van Fossen takes a middling position about the possible reworking of the text by a writer other than Marlowe. Textual and explanatory notes run below text.

Tamburlaine the Great

39. Brown, John Russell, introd. *Tamburlaine the Great Parts I and II.* London: Rex Coggings, Ltd., 1976.
    National Theatre Group acting version of the plays;

modern-spelling edition based on the 1590 text with scenes cut
indicated at end.

40. Harper, J. W., ed. *Tamburlaine.* (New Mermaids) London:
    Benn, and New York: Hill & Wang, 1971. 175 pp.
    A scholarly edition following the format of the series: critical
introduction, note on text, explanatory and textual notes running
below the printed texts of the two parts of *Tamburlaine.*

41. Jump, John D., ed. *Tamburlaine the Great, Parts I and II.*
    (Regents Renaissance Drama Series) Lincoln: University of
    Nebraska Press, 1967. xxvi + 205 pp.
    In his critical introduction the editor concludes that "We
may legitimately have our doubts about the ethics of the play in
which Marlowe's Tamburlaine is held up for our almost unbounded admiration; but we can have no doubts about our im-
mediate, spontaneous sympathy with the eager aspiration that was
so important a part of what Marlowe was trying to express
through him" (p. xxii). Textual and explanatory notes running
concurrently below plays.

42. Marlowe, Christopher. *Tamburlaine the Great.* Menston,
    Yorkshire: Scholar Press, 1973.
    Facsimile of the first edition printed by Richard Jones,
1590.

43. Ribner, Irving, ed. *Christopher Marlowe's Tamburlaine the
    Great Part I and Part II: Text and Major Criticism.*
    "Foreword" by Kenneth Friedenreich. Indianapolis: Odyssey
    Press, 1974. xi + 356 pp.
    Reprints texts of the two parts with notes from Ribner's
1963 edition of the *Complete Plays.* Reprints articles by Ethel
Seaton, "Marlowe's Map"; Roy W. Battenhouse, "Tamburlaine,
the 'Scourge of God'"; Helen Gardner, "The Second Part of
Tamburlaine the Great"; G. I. Duthie, "The Dramatic Structure
of *Tamburlaine the Great,* Parts I & II"; Clifford Leech "The
Structure of Tamburlaine"; Robert Kimbrough, "*I Tamburlaine:* A
Speaking Picture in a Tragic Glass"; Susan Richards, "Marlowe's
Tamburlaine II: A Drama of Death"; "Language and Action in
Marlowe's *Tamburlaine*" by David Daiches, from his Sorbonne
lecture, 1961. Also excerpts from books by Ellis-Fermor and

Eugene M. Waith. The volume also includes a new essay, "Directions in Tamburlaine Criticism," by Kenneth Friedenreich, pp. 341–352, plus an extensive, unannotated bibliography, pp. 353–56.

44. Wolff, Tatiana A., ed. *Tamburlaine the Great, Parts I and II.* London: Methuen & Co. 271 pp.
    An edition for the general reader.

CONCORDANCES

45. Crawford, Charles. *The Marlowe Concordance.* 2 vols. 1911–1932; reprinted New York: Burt Franklin, 1964.
    Still valuable, to be superseded by Robert Fehrenbach's Concordance of the *Works,* a computer-prepared version following the new Bowers text of the *CW* [See 8 above, I, x–xi.]

46. Ule, Louis and Hirschmann, Rudolf. *The Marlowe Concordance.* Georg Olms Verlag. [In progress at this time; to appear April, 1979.]
    According to Professor Ule, the new concordance will be a KWOC—key word out of context—type. It will be a modern-spelling concordance; it will include "alphabetized listings of all words with specific act, line, and scene designations;... variant readings; tables of syntactical quantity and distribution; and listings of word frequencies. [Additional information prior to publication can be obtained from the Marlowe Society of America, c/o Jean Jofen, President, Baruch College, 17 Lexington Avenue, New York, N.Y. 10010. See the Society's "Newsletter" for June, 1977, pp. 1–2 and p. 5.]

Syntax

47. Ando, Sadao. *A Descriptive Syntax of Christopher Marlowe's Language.* Tokyo: University of Tokyo Press, 1976. 721 pp.
    An impressive post-Chomskian grammar and syntax analysis of Marlowe's work.

2. GENERAL STUDIES ABOUT MARLOWE

48. Alexander, Claudia Borello. "Gentillet and Marlowe: A Study of the Historical Origins and Significance of the Machiavel. *DAI*, 37 (1977), 5839 A.

48a. Alexander, Peter. "Shakespeare, Marlowe's Tutor." *TLS*, 2 April, 1964, p. 280.
   Argues that in *Edward II*, Marlowe is imitating the second and third parts of *Henry VI;* that Marlowe's "judicious" handling of history in *Edward II* was learned from Shakespeare's use of the Chronicles in his plays. The evidence would suggest that Shakespeare, Marlowe (and Kyd, too) were all associated with Pembroke's Men in 1592.

49. Alton, R. E. "Marlowe Authenticated." *TLS*, 26 April, 1974, pp. 446–447. [See also Roma Gill, *TLS*, 3 May: 477: Fredson Bowers, *TLS*, 10, May: 502; Keith Walker, *idem.;* R. E. Alton, *TLS*, 17 May, 528; P. Daley, *TLS*, 14 June, 641.]
   Series of letters ostensibly beginning as a comment on Marlowe's signature as it relates to Bowers' edition [8], but which becomes an exchange of letters, pro and con, about the value of the edition, overall.

50. Amoruso, Vito. *"The Tragic Glass:* L'avventura drammatica di Christopher Marlowe." *Trimestre,* 3 (1969), 466–493; 4 (1970), 195–222. [In Italian]

51. Annis, Leroy E. "Christopher Marlowe's Multiple Perspective: The Source of Dramatic Ambivalence." *DAI,* 30 (1969), p. 1975A. (University of Washington)

52. Anonymous. "Marlowe and the Absolute." *TLS,* 24 February, 1956, p. 116.
   Justly celebrates the power of Marlowe's poetry, where

"ever and again there flashes out the illumining image or
passionate line, releasing or refreshing the imagination, either by
the swing of the phrase or the inspired precision of the word."

53. Anzai, Tetsuo. "Marlowe and Machiavelli." *Sophia: Studies
    in Western Civilization and Cultural Interaction of East and
    West*, 19 (1970), 27–50.
    Marlowe's use of Machiavelli's ideas represent the dynamic
example of the influence of thought by one author upon another.

54. Artemel, S. "'Where the Turk's Horse Once Treads'." *Notes
    and Queries*, N.S. 18 (1971), 216–223.
    Suggests the adaptation of the proverb by Marlowe in *1
Tamburlaine* (III.i.50–55) that "Where the Turk's horse once
treads, the grass no longer grows." Marlowe alludes to this commonplace to show the terror of the Turk and to upbraid Christians for their hypocrisy and factiousness. This is, moreover, an
important survey of Renaissance conceptions of the Turk and is of
general interest.

55. Ashe, Dora Jean. "The Non-Shakespearean Bad Quartos as
    Provincial Acting Versions." *Renaissance Papers*, 1 (1954),
    57–62.
    An analysis with slight reference to Marlowe that suggests
how provincial acting versions of Elizabethan plays might have
been arrived at by the company.

56. Asibong, Emmanuel Bassey. "Comic Sensibility in the Plays
    of Christopher Marlowe." *DAI* 36 (1976), 6108A.

57. Ayres, Philip J. "The Revision of 'Lust's Dominion'." *Notes
    and Queries*, NS 17 (1970), 212–213.
    Reviews questions of disputed authorship and revsions with
reference to Marlowe.

58. Bakeless, John. *Christopher Marlowe: The Man in His Time.*
    1937; rpt. New York: Washington Square Press, 1964. 335
    pp.
    Free-wheeling and speculative study designed to identify
the character of Marlowe the man as revealed in his plays.

59. Barber, Lester E. "A Recent Edition of Marlowe." *Research Opportunities in Renaissance Drama*, 17 (1974), pp. 17–24.

A review critical of the new edition by Bowers [8] because it merely reasserts old ideas about text and canon instead of breaking new ground; Barber also wonders how the volume can be of use to the general audience of readers without commentary and explanatory notes.

60. Barberena Blasquez, Elvia. *Christopher Marlowe. Su Vida y sus Obras Dramaticas*. Mexico City: Universidad Nacional Autonoma Facultad de Filosofia y Letras, 1952. 155 pp.

A general survey and characterization of Marlowe's life and works in Spanish; for Barberena Blasquez, Marlowe works subjectively. We find in his plays his glorification of individualism and independence. Close examination of them suggests the precise nature of his own beliefs; the situations of his plays reveal almost an existential consideration of religious and political problems.

61. Barker, Walter L. "The English Pantalones: A Study in Relations between the Commedia Dell'arte and Elizabethan Drama." *DAI*, 27 (1967), 3419A (University of Connecticut).

62. Baron, Mary K. "'The Meaning Has a Meaning': A Critical Reading of the Major Plays of Christopher Marlowe." *DAI*, 34 (1974), 7698A (University of Illinois: Champaign-Urbana)

63. Barrington, Michael. "Marlowe's Alleged Atheism." *Notes and Queries*, 195 (1950), 250–251 [and letter by Lynette and Eveline Feasey, *N&Q*, 195: 392–393].

"No atheist would have written a drama based on the question, "What will it profit a man to gain the world and lose his soul'?" [i.e., *Faustus*]. Barrington further maintains that Marlowe's "ardent sense of beauty" would argue against atheism. The Feaseys counter, arguing that Marlowe's religious beliefs are tinged with deep skepticism, as are those of his fellow Christian-humanist, George Chapman.

64. Battenhouse, Roy W. "Marlowe Reconsidered: Some Reflections on Levin's *Overreacher*." *Journal of English and Germanic Philology*, 52 (1953), 531–542. [See entry 156.]

Review essay asserting that Marlowe's atheism is dramatic, not literal. Battenhouse says that Levin and others assert naturalism in Marlowe, while they basically ignore "his implicit moral and ontological structures, his artistic balances, his faithfulness to the dramatic mode, and his grand designs" (p. 542).

65. Bawcutt, N. W. "James Broughton's Edition of Marlowe's Plays." *Notes and Queries*, NS 18 (1971), 449–452.

Among 1818 edition plays known to have been edited by Broughton, his *Jew of Malta* displays "his useful work in sorting out location, marking of asides, and the attribution of speeches." His *Dido* may be the first modern reprinting of the play.

66. Bevington, David M. *From Mankind to Marlowe: Growth of Structure in the Popular Drama of Tudor England.* Cambridge, Massachusetts: Harvard University Press, 1962. Reprinted 1968. viii + 310 pp.

An informative and seminal study of Marlowe's dramatic traditions and the conditions of production in the Tudor Age. Chapters give some idea of the scope of the book: From *Mankind* to Marlowe; Criteria for Popular Repertory; Auspices for the Elite Drama; The Popular Canon; "Four Men and a Boy"; The Traditions of Versatility; Doubling Patterns in the 1580's and 1590's; The Origins of Popular Dramatic Structure; The Pioneering Contributions of Bale and Skelton; The Intermediate Morality; Repetition, Expansion, and Elaboration; Dual Protagonists and a Formula for Homiletic Tragedy; The Expansion to Chronicle; The Transition to Romance; *Tamburlaine the Great; The Jew of Malta; Edward II;* The *Conflict of Conscience* and *Doctor Faustus.* Appendix: Plays "Offered for Acting"; The Texts of the Plays; Bibliography.

Bevington contends that there exists a close connection between Marlowe's dramas and earlier Tudor interludes and moral plays, which explains in part the ambiguities of purpose and impact in *Tamburlaine* and *The Jew of Malta* especially. Links to the early drama in *Tamburlaine* are manifest in episodic plot-development, symmetrical relations of scenes, and expansion of the cast "by references to invisible presences." In *The Jew of Malta,* this continuity is found in acts of evil intensified "by repeated example." In *Edward II,* casting suppression serves to "highlight a particular phase in the careers of the protagonists";

the play is not morally ambiguous. In *Doctor Faustus* (implicitly Marlowe's final play), Marlowe attains "a vital fusion of secular subject and traditional form." It is attained by seeing the comic scenes as an integral part of the drama, treating Faustus' sins "satirically"; by symmetrical balance of good and evil characters; but finally, by a recognition of Faustus' "representative human predicament." In Marlowe, Bevington concludes, a new age of drama, secular and moral, begins. While at times Bevington's structural emphasis may cause us to lose sight temporarily of other elements of the plays, such as language and spectacle, and while at times it appears that the author believes all dramatists were subordinate to the conditions of their respective companies, the work is deserving of its high esteem in Marlowe studies.

Reviews include: *Theatre Arts*, 46:4 (1962), 190; *TLS*, 10 August, 1962, 500.

67. Black, Matthew. "Enter Citizens." In *Studies in the English Renaissance Drama dedicated to the Memory of Karl Julius Holzknecht.* J. W. Bennett, Oscar Carghill, and Vernon Hall, eds. New York: New York University Press, 1959, pp. 16–27.

Shows that background figures in stage action, such as sailors, watchmen, citizens—termed "numeraries"—originate in the craft cycle plays. Among Renaissance dramatists "Marlowe has a stronger feeling for his minor personages" than is usually supposed, as, for instance, the three Jews who function as foils to Barabas, Faustus' two "pious friends," and the murderers in *The Massacre at Paris.*

68. Boas, Frederick S. *Christopher Marlowe: A Biographical and Critical Study.* 1940; rev. ed. Oxford: Clarendon Press, 1953. xvi + 336 pp.

After nearly four decades, still the standard biography; judicious and conservative in approach to the man, career, and writings.

69. Bobin, Donna. "Marlowe's Humor." *Massachusetts Studies in English*, 2 (1969), 29–40.

Old king and authority figures are ridiculed in the early plays (i.e., *Tamburlaine*), whereas in later ones (i.e., *Massacre, Edward II*, and *Faustus*), the hero is also subject to humorous detraction, suggesting Marlowe's maturing artistic vision.

70. Böhm, Rudolf. "Die Marlowe-Forschung der letzten beiden Jahrzehnten." *Anglia*, 88 (1965), 324–343; 454–470. [In German]

A lengthy survey of scholarship and criticism since the end of the second World War.

71. Box, Terry J. "Irony and Objectivity in the Plays of Christopher Marlowe." *DAI*, 33 (1973), 4333A–4334A (Texas Tech.)

Reacting to the currents of interpretation that see Marlowe as a subjective artist who identifies with his heroes, this writer argues for his ironic detachment from both their aspirations and failures.

72. Bradbrook, Frank W. "Marlowe and Keats." *Notes and Queries*, NS 5 (1958), 97–98.

Keats' *Ode to Melancholy* influenced by the Helen episode in *Doctor Faustus*.

73. Bradbrook, Muriel C. *English Dramatic Form: A Study of Its Development*. London: Chatto & Windus, 1965.

Chapter Three (pp. 41–61) deals with Marlowe's "dramatic inheritance"; the author believes that his stage is still conceived of as if it were open air in the sense of the earlier pageants and cycle plays; Marlowe's acting conventions are therefore more "primitive" than in the early plays of Shakespeare, with Marlowe's emphasis and movement from one long set speech to another.

74. ———. *Themes and Conventions of Elizabethan Tragedy*. 1935; rpt. Cambridge: Cambridge University Press, 1966. viii + 275 pp.

A "must" for new students of the subject, especially the first half of the book, which explains the practices and conventions of the dramatists at large (pp. 1–136). Survey of Marlowe's plays (pp. 137–164) is less convincing, but few would disagree with her final assessment of his work: "It is evident that Marlowe was developing very rapidly, both technically and in the more important senses. It might even be hazarded that he was developing towards a more 'Shakespearean' (that is, more inclusive) style, for in *Edward II* there can be found the most formalised qualities of feeling, and the most naturally human" (p. 164).

75. Breit, Harvey. "Shakeslowe." *New York Times Book Review,* 23 January, 1955, p. 8.

A lively, general view of the controversy over the author-ship of Shakespeare's plays in light of the publication of Calvin Hoffman's *The Death of the Man Who Was Shakespeare* [130].

76. Brooke, Nicholas. "Marlowe as a Provocative Agent in Shakespeare's Early Plays." *Shakespeare Survey,* 14 (1961), pp. 34–44.

Sees Shakespeare responding to the implicit assumptions in the moral positions of Marlowe's overreaching heroes in his own early histories and tragedies. Repulsed by the villany of Mar-lowe's heroes, Shakespeare's villains, notably Aaron in *Titus Andronicus* and Richard III, exhibited duality of purpose.

77. ———. "Marlowe the Dramatist." In *Elizabethan Theatre.* (Stratford-upon-Avon Studies, 9) John Russell Brown and Bernard Harris, eds. London: Edward Arnold and New York: St. Martin's Press, 1966, pp. 86–105.

A very important essay arguing that the controversies sur-rounding Marlowe's life and his alleged beliefs have obscured his real contribution to the stage of his time and afterwards. Mar-lowe, Brooke believes, "was exploiting the potentialities of exist-ing dramatic forms," a task that "though it calls for creative intel-ligence, does not require total planning from scratch; rather, it supposes imaginative opportunism and might well produce a re-sult more complex than the intention" (p. 104).

78. Brooks, Harold. "Marlowe and Early Shakespeare." In *Christopher Marlowe,* pp. 67–94. (Mermaid Critical Commen-taries) Edited by Brian Morris. [See entry 170.]

Marlowe's influences are seen in his use of traditional native dramatic forms; his classical learning; the ability of having charac-ters speak their minds directly; the conception of the aspiring hero; possibly the concept of the "scourge of God" as a Renais-sance commonplace he dramatized. While Brooks is aware of the interactions and influence, he observes that Marlowe's bequest to Shakespeare was unique in that he alone among the popular dramatists of the day was a poetic dramatist of genius.

79. Brown, John Russell. "Marlowe and the Actors." *Tulane Drama Review,* 8:4 (1964), 155–173.

Argues that the actors were subordinate to the overall conception of the play as a whole idea. Unlike Shakespeare, therefore, Marlowe does not develop his characters, a fact which requires an entirely distinct approach for actors playing Marlovian roles.

80. Brown, William J. "From Persepolis to Cyprus: The Disintegration of the Self-Contained Military Hero in Marlowe and Shakespeare." *DAI*, 27 (1967), 3421A (Duke University)
    With especial emphasis on *Tamburlaine*.

81. Butrym, Alexander. "A Marlowe Echo in Kyd." *Notes and Queries*, NS 5 (1958), 96–97.
    Spanish Tragedy IV.iv, 176–83 alludes to *Faustus*, III. iii, 327–8: "Had I as many lives as there be starres" from "Had I as many soules, as there be starres."

82. Bynum, James J., Jr. "Isolation, Metamorphosis, and Self-Destruction in the Plays of Christopher Marlowe." *DAI*, 34 (1973), 719A–720A (Emory University)

83. Carpenter, Nan C. "A Reference to Marlowe in Charles Butler's *Principles of Musick* (1636)." *Notes and Queries* 198 (1953), 16–18.
    A likely pejorative allusion to Marlowe in a passage on sacred music where Butler says that "now our Marlowes are turned to Quarleses," as if to suggest the transformation from writing profane to sacred music. The reference adds to Marlowe's early posthumous reputation in "the depths of opprobrium."

84. Chang, Joseph S. "'Of Mighty Opposites': Stoicism and Machiavellism." *Renaissance Drama*, 9 (1966), 37–57.
    Argues that doctrines of Stoicism such as patience in the face of adversity and adherence to virtue by individuals are often countered in Renaissance plays by the cynical and opportunistic notions of Elizabethan-distilled Machiavellian ideas. While many have noted each in plays, Chang argues the two appear in tandem as foils for each other; some passing reference to Marlowe.

85. Clarke, Peter P., II. "The Pastoral/Anti-Pastoral Dialectic in the Plays of Christopher Marlowe." *DAI*, 32 (1972), 5176A (University of Massachusetts)

86. Clay, Charlotte N. *The Role of Anxiety in English Tragedy: 1580-1642.* (Salzburg Studies in English Literature under the Direction of Professor Erwin A. Stürzl. Jacobean Drama Studies, No. 23) Editor: James Hogg. Salzburg: Institut für Englische Sprache und Literatur, 1974. 251 pp.

An historical consideration of the problem of Angst in the drama. While definitions are derived from the era of post-Renaissance thought by necessity (p. 3), Clay sees the Reformation as largely responsible for the destruction of integral wholeness that medieval thinkers adhered to. Chapter IV deals with Marlowe (pp. 87-114), especially with Tamburlaine and Faustus. Clay declares that "Marlowe took a long step forward in changing the concept of tragedy" by stimulating "a desire for the portrayal of ambition" by later dramatists with greater psychological complexity (p. 106). Further, through Marlowe's treatment, "Death became less a 'dance macabre' or a morality summons and more an awareness of nonbeing or nothingness. The anxiety of the age forced the dramatist to consider questions basic to man's being" (p. 114).

87. Clemen, Wolfgang, *English Tragedy before Shakespeare.* Translated by T. S. Dorsch. London: Methuen & Co., 1961. 301 pp.

Marlowe's contribution to tragedy is the focus on a single idea, embodied by his protagonist, "round whom the whole action and all the other characters revolve" (p. 113). In *Tamburlaine* Marlowe achieved an essential, successful "combination of language, stage-tableau, and action" (p. 129); whereas in his later work he is able to achieve a directness of address that reveals the inner conflicts of his protagonists (pp. 141-162). Clemen's survey of English tragedy is a valuable beginning place for students of the subject; general enough to provide an overview of the main contours of the subject in its time; specific enough to make particular and keen passing observations about individual authors.

88. ———. "Shakespeare and Marlowe." In *Shakespeare, 1971: Proceedings of the World Shakespeare Congress, Vancouver, August, 1971.* Cliffored Leech and J. M. R. Margeson, eds. Toronto: University of Toronto Press, 1971. Pp. 123-132.

A comparison between dramatic styles in *Edward II* and *Richard II;* the former notable for direct language and conflict of character; the latter for suggestive, highly metaphorical language, ritual, and gradual revelation of character.

89. Cole, Douglas. "Christopher Marlowe, 1564–1964, A Survey." *Shakespeare Newsletter,* 14 (1964), 44.
    Brief survey of major developments in Marlowe studies.

90. ————. *Suffering and Evil in the Plays of Christopher Marlowe.* Princeton: Princeton University Press, 1962; reprinted, New York: Gordian Press, 1974. x + 274 pp.
    Identifies suffering and evil as the principal problems in the world of Marlowe's plays and in his conception of drama; he interprets plays thematically in a Christian frame of reference: "In trying to define the characteristic dramaturgical and ideological dimensions of Marlowe's portrayal of suffering and evil, one is struck at first by the sheer diversity of technique and attitude exhibited in such a small body of work. The exploitation of staged physical violence ranges from the wholesale slaughter of *The Massacre at Paris* to the single 'hellish fall' of Doctor Faustus. . . ."
    Reviews include Irving Ribner, *Journal of English and Germanic Philology,* 62 (1963), 378–380; W. F. McNeir, *Criticism,* 5: 372–376; and Michel Poirer, *Études Anglaises,* 16 (1963), 73–74.

91. Cornelius, Richard M. "Marlowe's Use of the Bible." *DAI,* 32 (1972), 912A–913A. (University of Tennessee)

92. Cox, C. B. "Brutalities of Power." *Spectator,* 4 September, 1964, pp. 313–314.
    Review of Marlowe studies by J. B. Steane and A. L. Rowse. Cox argues that Marlowe explores the fascist impulse to unlimited power in the early plays, but moves to a more ambiguous view of power in later works, especially *Edward II.*

93. Cross, Gustav. "The Authorship of *Lust's Dominion.*" *Studies in Philology,* 55 (1958), 39–61.

93a. ————. "The Vocabulary of Lust's Dominion."
    Neuphilologische Mitteilungen, 58 (1958), 41–48.
    Both articles seek to disprove Francis Kirkman's seventeenth-century attribution of the work to Marlowe, advocating instead John Marston's considerable share in it.

94. Crutwell, Patrick. *The Shakespearean Moment and Its Place in the Poetry of the Seventeenth Century.* London: Chatto & Windus, 1954. 262 pp.
   An intriguing and sensitive treatment of influence and literary interactions; some reference to Marlowe.

95. Cutts, John P. *The Left Hand of God: A Critical Interpretation of the Plays of Christopher Marlowe.* Haddonfield, N.J.: Haddonfield House, 1973. 254 pp.
   Argues unconvincingly that all of Marlowe's heroic protagonists are effeminate, underreachers; all are ironically weak men, overtly or covertly homosexual. Conversely, Marlowe's women are usually viragos. There are worthwhile observations throughout this book, unfortunately subordinated to its author's *outré* perception of Marlowe. Reviews in *Choice*, 11 (June, 1974), 589; *Library Journal*, 99 (15 May, 1974), 1390; and *Criticism*, 17 (1975), 366.

96. ———. "The Marlowe Canon." *Notes & Queries*, NS 6 (1959), 71–74.
   The allusions in the Prologue to *Doctor Faustus*, may include references not to *Edward II* and *Tamburlaine*, but rather to a play (or plays) about Hannibal and Scipio. These plays on classical themes antedate *Tamburlaine*.

97. d'Agostino, Nicola. *Christopher Marlowe, studio.* Rome: Edizioni di Storia e Letteratura, 1950. 111 pp.
   Sees Marlowe's dramatic world as infused by the vitality of great solitary, individual characters, through which he explores the extremes of failure and achievement in human potential; his characters embody ideas rather than live them; for instance the relationship between Tamburlaine and Zenocrate idealizes the connection between Beauty and Poetry and has little connection with human passions of ordinary mortals: "esso ha poco della umana corrispondeza di due anime" (23). Extensive bibliography of English and Italian studies until 1950. Foreword by Mario Praz.

98. Dameron, J. Lasley. "Marlowe's 'Ships of War'." *American Notes and Queries*, 2 (1963), 19–20.
   Allusions in *Faustus* and *Jew of Malta* are topical and refer to Spanish naval threat posed by Armada to England.

99. Das, Sisr Kamar. "Christopher Marlowe and the Modern
Reader." *Bulletin of the Department of English: Calcutta*, 6:3
(1970–1971), 7–14.
Marlowe's heroes are champions of their own destinies, not
merely moral exempla. Marlowe is a modern because his plays
explore the polarities in human experience between unbounded
potential and man's very real limitations.

100. Denonian, Jean-Jacques. "Christopher Marlowe, dramaturge
'en mage'?" *Caliban*, 10 (1974), 57–76. [In French]
Both this and the following essay develop the idea that
Marlowe was not an atheist, but rather a deist and that the position is displayed in his dramas.

101. ———. "Un nomme Christopher Marlowe, Gentleman."
Caliban, 1 (1964), 51–74.

102. Dent, R. W. "Ovid, Marlowe, and *The Insatiate Countess*."
Notes & Queries, NS 10 (1963), 324–325.
The Insatiate Countess draws at several places from Ovid's
Elegies as translated by Marlowe. These are I.viii,43; I.viii,113–
114; II.ix,29–34; II.ix,37–38; and III.ii,33–34.

103. Dick, Bernard F. "A Marlovian Source for Belladonna's
Boudoir: *The Wasteland*, 77–100." *T. S. Eliot Newsletter*,
1:1 (1974), 2–3.
Eliot inverts Temple of Venus from *Hero and Leander*.

104. Doran, Madeleine. *Endeavours of Art: A Study of Form in
Elizabethan Drama*. Madison: University of Wisconsin
Press, 1954; reprinted 1963 and 1972. xiii + 482 pp.
An ambitious and valuable study with considerable emphasis on Marlowe's major dramas; its aims are best set out by
Doran herself:
"The present book will seek to define and examine the
problems of form that Shakespeare and his fellow dramatists had
to face and try to solve. It will attempt, as has been said, to
reconstruct imaginatively some part of the context of artistic
ideas, attitudes, tastes, and interests in which they worked, and
to define their problems in the light of these. The discussion will
be centered on Shakespeare's period, beginning with his im-
mediate predecessors, and ending with the Jacobeans who were

at least starting to write before his death. There will be presented, first, a set of limiting renaissance attitudes towards and ideas about literary art generally, then the important ideas about the drama particularly, and finally, resulting from these, a set of problems faced by dramatists in writing their plays. The first three chapters are general. 'Eloquence' is treated first because it seems to be the major defining characteristic of renaissance literature. Next comes a cluster of related ideas (imitation, verisimilitude, decorum), followed by the didactic theory of poetry; these ideas are the general principles in terms of which the Renaissance sees its literary problems. After these general matters come specific problems of the drama: first, the concepts of kinds of drama, and the conflicts revealed between inherited conventional forms and the development of new ones; next, problems of character (varying conceptions of character, modes of depiction, techniques of motivation); then, problems of plot construction (the problem of securing unity without sacrificing the variety the taste of the age demanded, and the problem of securing coherence in adapting episodic narrative to drama); finally, the problem of achieving form adequate to meaning—in short, the problem of successful artistic creation." (p. 23).

105. Dunn, Hough-Lewis. "The Language of the Magician as Limitation and Transcendance in the Wölfenbuttel *Faustbuch*, Greene's *Friar Bacon*, Marlowe's *Faustus*, Shakespeare's *The Tempest*, and Goethe's *Faust*." *DAI*, 35 (1974), 444A–445A. (University of Texas, Austin)

106. Eagle, Roderick. "The Mystery of Marlowe's Death." *Notes and Queries*, 197 (1952), 399–402.
    Claims that Marlowe was murdered, perhaps for reasons of counter-espionage, and that the Coroner's investigation, by its laxity, may be reason to suspect that he was acting in accordance with the wishes of the Privy Council.

107. Ellis-Fermor, Una M. "Marlowe and Green: A Note on Their Relations as Dramatic Artists." In *Studies in Honor of T. W. Baldwin*, pp. 136–149. D. C. Allen, ed. Urbana: University of Illinois Press, 1958.
    Suggestive paper that finds Greene's artistic habits of imitation resulting in severe difficulties in terms of language, con-

ception, and execution of dramatic ideas because of Marlowe's successes; Ellis-Fermor maintains that only in *Friar Bacon* can we observe "the maturity of Greene's art, the security alike of his humor and of his romance" (145). These are qualities of his "native genius" that are evident when he emancipates himself from attempts at imitating Marlowe's poetic and dramatic effects.

108. Ericson, Elmer H. "Christopher Marlowe: Human Affection in His Major Plays." *DAI*, 32 (1971), 1468A. (Utah)

109. Erlich, Richard D. "Wise Men and Fools: Values and Competing Theories of Wisdom in a Selection of Tragedies by Tourneur, Marlowe, Chapman, and Shakespeare." *DAI*, 32 (1972), 5735A. (University of Illinois)

110. Fanta, Christopher G. *Marlowe's 'Agonists': An Approach to the Ambiguity of His Plays.* (LeBaron Russell Briggs Prize Honors Essays in English, 1970) Cambridge, Massachusetts: Harvard University Press, 1970. 60 pp.
    A challenging brief study which claims that the major problem in the interpretations of the plays is their ambiguity. Fanta sees a progressive development in Marlowe regarding the handling of "agonists," somewhat in the Greek sense but moreover in terms of suffering and pathos. Our sympathies are divided between Marlowe's heroes and their victims, though his heroes are in part victims themselves.

111. Finnegan, Dana G. "The Development of Marlowe's Dramatic Skills." *DAI*, 29 (1969), 3608A–3609A. (University of Missouri, Columbia)

112. Fraser, Russell. "On Christopher Marlowe." *Michigan Quarterly Review*, 12 (1973), 136–159.
    A general survey of Marlowe's achievement as dramatist and thinker: his plays repeatedly engage audiences because of their ambiguous moral impact and in showing the pointlessness of violence. Marlowe's greatest fusion of these concepts occurs in *Edward II*.

113. Freeman, Arthur. "Marlowe, Kyd, and the Dutch Church Libel." *English Literary Renaissance*, 3 (1973), 44–52.

Reproduces the text of a 53-line poem, hitherto unknown save for four lines, that strengthens the evidence indicating Marlowe was a target of the Privy Council in the spring of 1593, and not implicated by Kyd as is usually believed. Because Marlowe was out of London when the Libel appeared, he was eventually set free.

114. Fried, David G. "Marlowe's Use of the Idea of Order." *DAI*, 32 (1971), 1470A. (New York University)

115. Frye, Roland Mushat. "Theological and Non-Theological Structures in Tragedy." *Shakespeare Studies*, 4 (1968), pp. 132–48.
    See especially pp. 134–39, which deal with *Faustus* and *Macbeth*. Frye sees Marlowe's play as inherently theological, where the demonic activity is overt (not, as in *Macbeth*, internalized in the hero's mind). Marlowe spells out the damnation of Faustus. In Christian tragedy all of the major incidents of the drama, as well as its language, the internal struggles of characters, are related to the overriding theological framework.

116. Garber, Marjorie. "'Infinite Riches in a Little Room': Closure and Enclosure in Marlowe." In *Two Renaissance Mythmakers: Christopher Marlowe and Ben Jonson*, pp. 3–21. (Selected Papers from the English Institute, 1975–76. New Series, No. 1) Edited, with a Foreword, by Alvin Kernan. Baltimore and London: The Johns Hopkins University Press, 1977.
    Perceptive general study of Marlowe's dramatic technique: Marlowe creates verbal and physical enclosures to "the pattern of meaning generated by the plays that contain them" (p. 15). As he encloses his characters in the mazes of their own actions and choices, Marlowe discloses meaning to the audience.

117. George, J. "An Allusion to Marlowe." *Notes and Queries*, 195 (1950), 138–139.
    In *The Cobbler's Prophecy* of Robert Wilson, II, 460–467.

118. Giamatti, A. Bartlett. "Marlowe: The Arts of Illusion." *Yale Review*, 61 (1972), 530–543.
    An interesting essay on the notion that Renaissance men

saw their power deriving from language; Marlowe in his whole career as a dramatist "wrestled with the multi-form angel (or demon) of language. He made his problem as a playwright the subject of his plays. He expanded the limits of the stage by writing of the human mind in its battle to surpass human limitation." Of his plays, especially *"Doctor Faustus* fully exploits the glories and terrors in language to illuminate the full ambiguity of the human condition . . . " (p. 534).

119. Gibson, H. N. *The Shakespeare Claimants: A Critical Survey of the Four Principal Theories Concerning the Authorship of Shakespearean Plays.* 1962; reprint ed., New York: Barnes & Noble, and London: Methuen & Co, 1971.
   A survey of the cases for Bacon, the Earls of Oxford and Derby, and Christopher Marlowe. Bibliography.

120. Godshalk, William L. *The Marlovian World Picture.* The Hague: Mouton, 1974. 244 pp.
   An intelligent study that seeks to establish a new terminology for Marlowe's dramatic achievement: "Marlowe was hardly the propagandist for Renaissance materialism, however romantic, colorful, and exciting that materialism may seem today. He appears most clearly as the incisive critic, with a full understanding of the vanity of human ambition. His vision is radical in its criticism, conservative in its nature. He is never a preacher, but always a seer, and his moral vision of the insanely aggressive world is turned to art. Along with this vision . . . his artistic strength is in 'monodrama' where the concentration is on the individual aspirer. . . . In the drama dominated by the central character, he could say most clearly what he had to say about human evil" (p. 37). In this approach Barabas and Faustus and Tamburlaine are given preeminence; the handling of Dido and Edward seem to fit less satisfactorily into his governing idea. Nonetheless, it is a readable, often perceptive study.

121. ———. "Marlowe, Milton, and the Apples of Hell." *Milton Quarterly,* 5 (1971), 34–35.
   Marlovian echo or source in *Paradise Lost.*

122. Goldman, Michael. "Marlowe and the Histrionics of Ravishment." *In Two Renaissance Mythmakers: Christopher*

Marlowe and Ben Jonson, pp. 22–40. (Selected Papers from
the English Institute. New Series, No. 1) Edited with a
foreword by Alvin Kernan. Baltimore & London: The Johns
Hopkins University Press, 1977.

Histrionics in Marlowe is the pattern of acting out emotions linking the central character to "objects in the world of the
play." The value given to some goal in the dramas, such as desire
for power in *Tamburlaine*, gold in *The Jew of Malta*, learning in
Faustus, Gaveston in *Edward II*, help to determine the structure
and development of the respective dramas, with this result: "the
hero effectively transforms something he loves into a source of
fear" (p. 35). A penetrating analysis of what constitutes in part
audience participation in Marlowe's plays.

123. Greenblatt, Stephen G. "Marlowe and Renaissance Self-
     Fashioning." In *Two Renaissance Mythmakers: Christopher
     Marlowe and Ben Jonson*, pp. 41–69. (Selected Papers from
     the English Institute, 1975–1976) Edited with a Foreword
     by Alvin Kernan. Baltimore and London: The Johns Hop-
     kins University Press, 1977.
     Follows the direction of this scholar's study of Ralegh. He
writes that "Marlowe is deeply implicated in his heroes, though
he is far more intelligent and self-aware than any of them. Cutting himself off from the comforting doctrine of repetition, he
writes plays that spurn and subvert his culture's metaphysical and
ethical certainties. . . . For the one true goal of all these heroes is
to be characters in Marlowe's plays; it is only for this, ultimately,
that they manifest their magnificent energy and their haunting
sense of longing" (pp. 63–64). Readers will note here the expression, in more sophisticated terms, of the late romantic conception
of Marlowe.

124. Gruninger, Hans W. "Brecht und Marlowe." *Comparative
     Literature*, 21 (1969), 232–244. [In German]
     Brecht's reworking of Marlowe's *Edward II*, though it
finds him speaking his own dramatic language, nonetheless owes
to his predecessor the figure of the "unfortunate Edward," whose
negative will and self-loathing lead him to the depths of suffering.

125. Harbage, Alfred. "Intrigue in Elizabethan Tragedy." In *Es-
     says on Shakespeare and Elizabethan Drama in Honor of*

Hardin Craig, pp. 37–44. Richard Hosley, ed. Columbia,
Missouri: University of Missouri Press, 1962.
The element of intrigue has been overlooked by students
of revenge plays; its result often is more comic than terrifying.
Some reference to Marlowe.

125a. Hawkins, Harriet. *Poetic Freedom and Poetic Truth.* Oxford: Oxford University Press, 1976. Pp. 135.
Contrasts Shakespeare and Marlowe in their creations of
characters who seem to fashion themselves and their roles in the
plays.

126. Henderson, Philip. *Christopher Marlowe.* London:
Longmans, Green, & Co., 1952; 2nd ed. New York and
Brighton: Barnes & Noble, Harvester Press, 1974. xxii +
162 pp.
Easily read account of Marlowe's life and work with an
emphasis on the sensational and lively, conjectural accounts of
Marlowe's espionage activities, "The School of Night," prison,
and the Privy Council. *Dido* is dismissed as an immature work;
Tamburlaine "illustrates the victory of the imagination over the
material world" but the hero degenerates in the second play into
megalomania; *The Jew of Malta* is flawed by a conception of
Barabas too immense for the action of the play to sustain; *The
Massacre at Paris* sees Machiavellianism as the instrument of the
Counter-Reformation; *Edward II* is perhaps his most mature
drama, in which, as in *Doctor Faustus*, "Marlowe showed that he
had become a master of the classic elements of tragedy—pity and
fear." Marlowe's approach to play writing is that of a lyric poet
who "had little interest in building up the successive stages of a
five-act drama." Rather, he was interested mostly in the central
idea of the play, and in the development of this end he is responsible for the invention of the dramatic monologue. Like many
early critics, Henderson sees Marlowe's heroes as the vehicles
who express his own beliefs.
Chapters: Canterbury; Cambridge; Government Service;
Newgate; The School of Night; The Shadow of the Star Chamber;
Deptford Strand; Drama; Hero and Leander; Marlowe as a
Dramatist.
Reviews include *The New Statesman and Nation,* 43 (29
March, 1952): 382; *Saturday Review,* 35 (12 July, 1952): 38; *TLS*
(23 May, 1952): 347.

127. ———. *Christopher Marlowe.* (Writers and Their Work, No. 81) London and New York, 1956; reprint Lincoln: University of Nebraska Press, 1962, with studies of Jonson, Webster, and Ford. Pp. 3–48.

    A boiled-down version of the author's 1952 study [entry 126].

128. ———. "Marlowe as a Messenger." *TLS*, 12 June, 1953, p. 381.

    Publishes a letter from Lord Cecil to Sir Henry Unton, delivered Dieppe by a certain "Mr. Marlin" on 16 March, 1592, providing evidence that Marlowe was at the siege of Rouen in that year.

129. Hilton, Delia. *Who Was Kit Marlowe? The Story of the Poet and Playwright.* London: Weidenfeld and Nicolson, 1977. xi + 163 pp.

    A lively and informal biography; the author has the annoying habit of referring to Marlowe throughout by the pet-name "Kit." In a tissue of loose conjecture, Hilton re-examines the important documents about Marlowe and speculates that he committed suicide for the flimsiest of reasons. General bibliography.

130. Hoffman, Calvin. *The Murder of the Man Who Was "Shakespeare."* New York: Messner, 1955. Reprinted New York: Grosset & Dunlap, 1960.

    Hoffman expected to find "Shakespeare" and the clue to his identity (Marlowe) in the Walsingham tomb. He contends that Marlowe was not killed on 30 May, 1593 in a tavern brawl, but was spirited away to the Continent where he wrote the Shakepeare canon.

    Reviews include *Time*, 65 (13 June, 1955): 108; *Saturday Review*, 38 (9 July, 1955): 16; and *Library Journal*, 80 (August, 1955): 1714; see also entry 75.

131. Homan, Sidney R. "Chapman and Marlowe: The Paradoxical Hero and the Divided Response." *Journal of English and Germanic Philology*, 68 (1969), 391–406.

    Marlowe's and Chapman's heroes are often possessed of extraordinary power and ability; yet, their often brutal behavior tends to divide audience reactions to them, which both dramatists intend to communicate their meanings. Marlowe is largely the innovator; Chapman extends the innovation.

132. Honey, William. *The Shakespeare Epitaph Deciphered.* London: Mitre Press, 1969.

Shakespeare died at Deptford (p. 214); the tomb at Stratford-upon-Avon contains the remains of Marlowe and the manuscripts of the works generally attributed to both men. A more "scholarly" verification of Hoffman's conclusions [see entry 130].

133. Hook, F. S. "Marlowe, Massinger, and Webster Quartos." *Notes and Queries,* NS 4 (1957), 64-65.

Describes holdings of the Honeyman Collection at Lehigh University.

134. Hotson, Leslie. "More Light on Shakespeare's Sonnets." *Shakespeare Quarterly,* 2 (1951), 111-118.

Argues for early date of sonnets, 1589; rival poet is unquestionably Marlowe.

134a. Hoy, Cyrus. "Shakespeare, Sidney, and Marlowe: The Metamorphoses of Love." *Virginia Quarterly Review,* 51 (1975), 448-458.

Unlike the heroes of Sidney and Shakespeare, Marlowe's protagonists are not transformed by the attributes of love and beauty rooted in poetic traditions, especially Ovid. Rather, they remain rigid, even isolated by the deterministic force of their own characters and personalities.

135. Hughes, Pennethorne. "The Vogue for Marlowe." *Month,* 8 (1952), 141-151.

Marlowe's appeal as modernist is the problem of power (p. 146); he was an intellectual revolutionary who dealt with issues of "theocracy, nationalism, and economics" in terms of individual heroes.

136. Jensen, Enjer J. "Marlowe Our Contemporary? Some Questions of Relevance." *College English,* 30 (1969), 627-632.

Addresses the problem of teaching Marlowe to American college students after the social unrest of the 1960s; manages an analogy between the social situation of Barabas in *The Jew of Malta* and social and racial discrimination of the "American Negro."

137. Kelly, Katherine A. "Legal Murder, Power Politics, and Elizabethan Tragedy." *DAI*, 32 (1972), 3954A–3955A. (University of Texas at Austin)

138. Klein, Donald S. "Symbolic Foreshadowing in the English History Play from *Gorboduc* to *Henry V*." *DAI*, 28 (1967), 2211A. (Pennsylvania State University)

139. Klein, John W. "Christopher Marlowe." *TLS*, 8 October, 1964, p. 924. See also Edward Fisher, *TLS*, 15 October, 1964, p. 939, and Klein again, 22 October, 1964, p. 959.
    Further discussion of Mercutio's identity with ad hoc support from Leslie Hotson (p. 924).

140. ———. "Was Mercutio Christopher Marlowe?" *Drama*, 60 (1961), 36–39.
    Evidence affirmative; the brawl of Act III of *Romeo and Juliet* is a version of the brawl in which William Bradley was killed by Marlowe after being attacked, with the intervention of his friend, poet Thomas Watson.

141. Knapp, Robert S. "The Coordinate Frame: Structure in English Drama 1580–1600." *DAI*, 29 (1969), 4493A. (Cornell)

142. Knights, L. C. "The Strange Case of Christopher Marlowe." In *Further Explorations*. Stanford: Stanford University Press, 1965, pp. 75–98.
    A thought-provoking assessment of Marlowe's place in English literature: he asked radical questions of a world where "self-righteous self-assurance . . . offered small resistance to drives for power and riches . . ." (81). Marlowe's assertive individual heroes nonetheless are exposed in their vulnerability by their creator; his religious beliefs are less the coolly detached reflections of a rationalist (Kocher, 1946) than of an engaged, exasperated mind. Knights believes Marlowe's work contains great verbal power, critical intelligence, "and conflicting emotions that were never quite clarified in a compelling dramatic image" (98).

143. Knoepfle, John I. "The Use of Renaissance Formulas for Praise in the Dramas of Christopher Marlowe." *DAI*, 28 (1968), 3148A (St. Louis)

144. Knoll, Robert E. *Christopher Marlowe*. (Twayne's English Authors Series, No. 74) New York: Twayne, 1969. 160 pp.
      Introduction to Marlowe's life and works in the standard Twayne format, including chronology, biography, and annotated bibliography of major primary and secondary works. Knoll rightly emphasizes Marlowe's maturation as a dramatist. *Tamburlaine* appeals because it capitalizes on the sensational; *Doctor Faustus*, here considered an early play, is divided artificially by the author to make thematic points about the human lust for unlimited power; *The Jew of Malta* and *The Massacre at Paris* are transitional works whose emphasis is on stage-business rather than central ideas; *Edward II* is divided into three sections representing the king's minion, his wars, and his death. *Edward II* is his most accomplished play and his most pessimistic one. *Hero and Leander* is a brilliant poem wherein the obtuseness of the narrator plays up Marlowe's theme of the "ironic disparity between experience and an account of it."
      Reviews include *Booklist*, 15 January 1970: 616. Among the introductory studies of Marlowe, this one is most free of cant and novelty for its own sake.

145. Kuehnert, Philip G. "Will and Fate in Four English Renaissance Tragedies." *DAI*, 35 (1974), 1626A. (University of Utah)

146. Kuriyama, Constance Brown. "Hammer or Anvil: A Psychoanalytic Study of the Plays of Christopher Marlowe." *DAI*, 34 (1974), 7710A. (University of California, Berkeley)

146a. Lalka, David George: "Christopher Marlowe: Some Studies in Genre." *DAI*, 37 (1977), 6501A.

147. Lambin, Georges. "Marlowe et la France." *Études Anglaises*, 19 (1966), 55–59. [In French]
      The assassination of Henry III in *Massacre* is based on actual French accounts and was not unduly exaggerated by Marlowe

in his play. Lambin conjectures Marlowe's familiarity with French materials may have come from his missions for Walsingham.

148. Lautenschlager, Peggy. "A Dramatization of the Life of Christopher Marlowe and a Play about a Modern Hero on the Theme: The Over-Reacher as Tragic Hero." *DAI*, 35 (1974), 3933A. (Brigham Young University) Soon to be a major motion picture?

149. Leech, Clifford. "The Acting of Marlowe and Shakespeare." The Second George Fullmer Reynolds Lecture for 1963; reprinted in *Colorado Quarterly*, 13:1 (1964), 25–42.

Both authors developed the formalized set speech beyond their predecessors; each uses comic scenes chorically. The power suggested in the eloquence of set speeches is consistently undermined in the latter comic exchanges, a situation of which actors must be aware.

150. ———. "Marlowe's Humor." In *Essays on Shakespeare and Elizabethan Drama in Honor of Hardin Craig*. Richard Hosley, ed. Columbia: University of Missouri Press, 1962, pp. 69–81. Reprinted in item 153 below, pp. 167–178.

A brief survey of the canon that suggests that Marlowe not only possessed a sense of humor, but it is manifested in his works both directly and by indirection: "The object of the present exercise has been to urge fuller recognition of the variety of Marlowe's humor, and its high degree of integration with the fabric of his writing." *Hero and Leander* is Marlowe's major comic work.

151. ———. "The Two-Part Play: Marlowe and the Early Shakespeare." *Shakespeare Jahrbuch*, 94 (1958), pp. 90–106.

Four modes of composition identified: one play (e.g., *Tamburlaine*) expanded into two parts; plays imitating this kind of work and divided into two parts (*Alphonsus, Selimus);* plays planned in two parts; plays with potential sequels.

152. ———. "When Writing Becomes Absurd." First of two George Fullmer Reynolds Lectures for 1963; reprinted in *Colorado Quarterly*, 13: 1 (1964), 3–24, and in *The Dramatist's Experience with other Essays in Literary Theory.*

London: Chatto & Windus and New York: Barnes and Noble, 1970, pp. 64–86.

Notes Marlowe's awareness of the central absurdity in the situations of his dramas: language and action can simultaneously glorify human endeavor, or display the tenuousness of man's place in the cosmos.

153. ———, ed. *Marlowe: A Collection of Critical Essays.*
(Twentieth Century Views Series) General Editor: Maynard Mack. Englewood Cliffs, New Jersey: Prentice Hall, 1964. 184 pp.

Reprints excerpts from early books and articles by Eliot, Seaton, Battenhouse, Greg, Ellis-Fermor, Wilson, Kocher, and from recent studies by Levin, Clemen, Brockbank, Bevington, Bradbrook, Waith, and Leech (see entry 150). Leech's critical introduction to the collection (pp. 1–11) is a survey of Marlowe's career and the complex responses that modern criticism has had to his work, ending with a call for greater investigation of the ways in which "eloquence and irony, word and visual effect, the comic and the tragic, are fused in his plays."

154. Leslie, Nancy T. "Marlowe in the Theater: 'Mark the Show'." *DAI*, 33 (1973), 5130A. (Emory University)

155. Levin, Harry. "Marlowe Today." *Tulane Drama Review*, 8:4 (1964), 22–31.

By affecting alienation in his plays, Marlowe's appeal is tempered to modern sensibilities rather than romantic ones.

156. ———. *The Overreacher: A Study of Christopher Marlowe.*
Cambridge, Massachusetts: Harvard University Press, 1952; reprinted, Boston: Beacon Press, 1964. xvi + 204 pp.

Arguably the single most important critical study of Marlowe during the period from 1950 to the present. He argues for a Marlowe in many respects quite similar to the romantic critics' view of him as a rebel, but with none of their quirks or excesses. Levin's Marlowe is a deeply and darkly intelligenced artist, whose tragic view is "The overreaching image, reinforced by the mighty line, [that] sums up the whole dramatic predicament and affords the actor a maximum of opportunity. The stage becomes a vehicle for hyperbole, not merely by accrediting the incredible or supporting rhetoric with a platform or sounding board, but by taking metaphors literally and acting concepts out. . . . Marlowe seems to have admired the ceremonies, if not dogmas, of the Catholic Church; and behind his plays, as behind all drama, loom the elemental configurations of ritual. . . . The unholy trinity of Marlowe's heresies, violating the taboos of medieval orthodoxy, was an affirmation of the strongest drives that animated the Renaissance and have shaped our modern outlook" (pp. 24, 26).

Chapters are "The End of Scholarism"; The Progress of Pomp; More of the Serpent; State Overturned; Science Without Conscience; The Dead Shepherd. There are nine appendices. Excerpts or whole chapters from the study have been reprinted elsewhere, including entries 33, 153, 193 and 378.

For reviews see entry 64 and the following: S. C. Chew, *New York Times Book Review*, 8 February, 1953, p. 3; R. A. Foakes, *Modern Language Notes*, 69 (1954), 123–125; Jean Jacquot, *Études Anglaises*, 8 (1954), 150–152; M. Ross, *Comparative Literature*, 7 (1955) 63–64; F. Wolcker, *Archiv*, 192:72; *Dalhousie Review*, 33:17; *Queen's Quarterly*, 59: 553–554; *University of Toronto Quarterly*, 24 (1955), 102–105.

157. Levin, Richard. *The Multiple Plot in English Renaissance Drama*. Chicago: University of Chicago Press, 1971. xiv + 277 pp.

A full-length seminal study about structures and functions of multiple plots in English drama, including short discussions of *Doctor Faustus* and *The Jew of Malta*.

158. McAleer, John J. "Marlowe's Solar Symbolism." *Drama Critique*, 3:3 (1960), 111–131.

Points out emblematic use of solar images in *Tamburlaine* and *Edward II* suggest on one hand protection of subjects and majesty; on the other hand a setting sun suggests man's challenges of divine order and authority and his consequent destruction (as in *Faustus*).

159. MacIntryre, James Malcolm. "Marlowe's Use of Rhetorical Figures." *DAI*, 23 (1963), 2518–2519. (University of Illinois)

160. Mahood, M. M. *Poetry and Humanism*. 1950; reprinted with corrections, New York: W. W. Norton & Co, 1970. 336 pp.

A wide-ranging study of seventeenth-century English literature in light of Renaissance humanism; Chapter III (pp. 54–86) is devoted to Marlowe's heroes. Mahood sees Marlowe reacting to the decadence of humanism in his plays; thus, rather than "advertising" the expansiveness of Renaissance aspirations, his heroes expose its limits. Some of her penetrating remarks have been reprinted elsewhere, including entries 37 and 193.

161. Margeson, J. M. R. *The Origins of English Tragedy.* Oxford: Clarendon Press, 1967. xiv + 194 pp.
A study of the "organizing and shaping principles by which dramatists over a period of time began to give their work tragic form" (p. iii). The greatest dramas of the English Renaissance, including *Faustus* and *Macbeth,* provide "a much more powerful and convincing view of the motives that drive men to ultimate decisions and rebellious or violent action." Frequent reference to Marlowe's major plays throughout.

162. Marion, Denis (pseudonym for Marion DeFosse). *Christopher Marlowe, dramaturge.* (Great Dramatists Series, No. 10) Paris: Arche, 1955. 156 pp. [In French]
Introduction to Marlowe's life and works.

162a. Martin, Richard Anderson, "The Theater of Experience: Dramatic Judgements in the Plays of Christopher Marlowe." *DAI* (1977), 5854A.

163. Masinton, Charles G. "Apollo's Laurel Bough: Essays on the Theme of Damnation in Christopher Marlowe." *DAI,* 27 (1967), 2133A–2134A. (University of Oklahoma)

164. ———. *Christopher Marlowe's Tragic Vision: A Study in Damnation.* Athens, Ohio: Ohio University Press, 1972. 168 pp.
"The central themes in Marlowe's plays reveal a preoccupation with the limitations inherent in man's abilities and corruption in both public and personal affairs. Marlowe finds in human nature a malignant destructive pride that manifests itself as political and moral degeneracy. Ironically, this degeneracy is the unavoidable result of man's attempt to realize full selfhood by presumptuously aspiring beyond the assumed limits of capabil-

ity. . . ." In this context, *Faustus* is his culminating statement, "the great-grandfather of the modern mentality that has produced the atomic bomb . . . and foreshadows the problem of the modern scholar or scientist whose intense specialization in one narrow discipline abstracts him completely from common human experience. . . ."

Chapters are The Tragic Glass; Tamburlaine and the Rhetoric of Persuasion; The Progress of His Pomp; The Death of Tamburlaine; Barabas and the Politics of Greed; Metamorphosis of Character in *Edward II;* Faustus and the Failure of Renaissance Man. Reviews include *Choice,* 10 (May, 1973): 458, and *Library Journal,* 98 (1 January, 1973): 71.

165. ———. "Marlowe's Artists: The Failure of Imagination." *Ohio University Review,* 11 (1969), 22–35.

Sees the heroes as victims of their own conceptions of what they desire to become; their "failures" are represented in their inabilities to realize their imagined potential.

166. Maxwell, J. C. "The Plays of Christopher Marlowe." In *The Age of Shakespeare.* Pelican Guide to English Literature, Vol. 2. General Editor: Boris Ford. Baltimore: Penguin Books, 1956; rev. 1963. Pp. 162–178.

General survey of Marlowe's works and assessment of his importance to English drama.

167. Meehan, Virginia M. "Christopher Marlowe, Poet and Playwright: Studies in Poetical Method." *DAI,* 27 (1967), 3432A, University of Florida.

168. ———. *Christopher Marlowe: Poet and Playwright—Studies in Poetical Method.* (De Proprietatibus Litterarum. Series Practica, 81) The Hague: Mouton, 1974. 100 pp.

Argues that Marlowe's imagery is not merely decorative, but functional, used, "especially in figures of speech, to affect the audience's emotions . . . (p. 10). As his poetical techniques developed Marlowe was able to appeal not only to the emotions (as in *Tamburlaine),* but to reason as well *(Edward II);* so that our perceptions and understandings of the plays are more complex; the figurative use of imagery is largely responsible for communicating Marlowe's deepening view of man.

169. Miller, J. Michael. "Marlowe 1964." *Clare Quarterly*, 11:4 (1964), 15–32.

   Evaluates Marlowe's place in English letters on the four-hundredth anniversary of his birth.

170. Morris, Brian, ed. *Christopher Marlowe: Mermaid Critical Commentaries*. London: Ernest Benn, 1968, and New York: Hill & Wang, 1969. x + 197 pp.

   Record of the York Symposium, held at Langwith College, University of York, 19 through 21 April, 1968, on Marlowe. Nine papers published in all, each of high quality and interest. All are annotated throughout this bibliography in appropriate places. See entries 78, 172, 181, 255, 273, 300, 322, 488, and 541.

171. Mortimer, Raymond. "Marlowe: English Genius of the Renaissance." The *Times* (London), 2 February, 1964, p. 35.

   Acknowledges his place in his own age and significance to ours on the occasion of the four-hundredth anniversary of his birth.

172. Mulryne, J. R. and Stephen Fender. "Marlowe and the 'Comic Distance'." In *Christopher Marlowe*, pp. 47–64 (Mermaid Critical Commentaries) Brian Morris, ed. [See entry 170.]

   Frequently in his plays Marlowe presents "contradictory views of experience [which] are brought together and left unresolved: the ideal and the common sense; the hint of a comprehensive order and the rejection of all order; the socially concerned and the individualist; the moral and the libertine; metaphor and fact" (p. 50). Marlowe is adept and unusual in his use of emblematic stage actions and language that help to effect our feelings of ambivalence to his characters; the essay deals primarily with *Dido, Tamburlaine*, and *Edward II*.

173. Mundy, P. D. "The Ancestry of Christopher Marlowe." *Notes and Queries*. NS 2 (1954), 328–331.

   Traces family back to the fifteenth century.

174. Norman, Charles. *Christopher Marlowe: The Muses' Darling*. 1946; revised, Indianapolis: Bobbs-Merrill Co., 1971. 273 pp.

Revision includes new information on Walsingham, Peele, Watson, notes have been expanded considerably. The book remains a romanticized approach to Marlowe's life and works.

175. Nozaki, Mutsumi. "The Comic Sense in Marlowe Reconsidered." *Shakespeare Studies*, 9 (1970–1971), 1–27. [Japan]
Copiously illustrates examples of the comic in Marlowe in urging critics and audiences to enlarge receptiveness to Marlowe's conscious humor.

176. Oliver, H. J. "Oxbury's Marlowe." *Notes and Queries*, NS 16 (1969), 287.
Oxbury seems to have edited four plays in 1818: *The Jew of Malta, Edward II, Doctor Faustus,* and *The Massacre at Paris. Tamburlaine* was edited in 1820; others apparently completed the set-edition.

177. O'Neill, Judith, ed. *Critics on Marlowe.* Coral Gables, Florida: University of Miami Press, 1970. 127 pp.
Reprints commentary from Renaissance to present; mostly brief excerpts, including Bradbrook (entry 74); Mahood (160); Levin (156); F. P. Wilson (237); Leech (328); N. Brooke (354); Brown (79); and Lewis (264).

178. Oras, Ants. "Lyrical Instrumentation in Marlowe: A Step Towards Shakespeare." *Studies in Shakespeare*, pp. 74–87. (University of Miami Publications in English and American Literature, No. 1) Coral Gables: University of Miami Press, 1953.
Deals with assonance in Marlowe's verse as it contributes to the music and power of the lines, spoken or read.

179. Ornstein, Robert. "*The Atheist's Tragedy.*" *Notes and Queries*, NS 3 (1955), 284–285.
Without claiming that Tourneur directly alludes to Marlowe or to *Doctor Faustus,* "it is not impossible that *The Atheist's Tragedy* reminded some Jacobeans that heavenly truth is stranger and more wonderful than impious fiction."

179a. Page, R. I. "Christopher Marlowe and Matthew Parker's Library." *Notes and Queries*, NS 24 (1977), 510–514.

Most scholars have taken for granted that Marlowe had access to the books in Matthew Parker's library, bequeathed by the Archbishop to Corpus Christi College following his death in 1578. Page suggests that in fact the library may not have been delivered until as late as 1593, the year of Marlowe's death. A second possibility is that though delivered in 1578, no register for the collection was made until 1593; a third, that the library was delivered by Parker's heir piecemeal over the same fifteen-year period. In any case "it is dangerous to assume that Marlowe saw any individual one of the Parker books and those who want to trace his intellectual development must seek elsewhere" (514).

180. Palmer, D. J. "Elizabethan Tragic Heroes." In *Elizabethan Theatre*, pp. 11–35 (Stratford-upon-Avon Studies, No. 9) John Russell Brown and Bernard Harris, eds. London: Edward Arnold, and New York: St. Martin's Press, 1966.
    A fine assessment of the conceptions of tragedy of Kyd and Marlowe; "Marlowe's drama is more intellectual and metaphysical than moral in its conception of human will and action. . . . No other Elizabethan is both as philosophical and exciting. . ." (p. 26). Unlike Shakespeare, however, Marlowe's tragic figures do not present values in their experiences which transcend mortality.

181. ———. "Marlowe's Naturalism." In *Christopher Marlowe*, pp. 151–175. (Mermaid Critical Commentaries) Brian Morris, ed. [See entry 170.]
    Marlowe's conception of his tragic plots is within the compass of "an empirical conception of natural causes" (p. 156); "Not only do his heroes refuse to obey any higher law than that of their own wills, but the course of their fortunes, even in death itself, insists only on a naturalistic plane of being upon which man subjectively imposes his own moral order" (*idem*). The naturalism which Marlowe subscribes to has complementary inspirations and sources in Ovid and Machiavelli. His "naturalism reflects his sophisticated and unusual approach to drama, his insistence on the autonomy of natural causes and his development of the ironic method of plot-construction represent an important contribution to . . . Elizabethan drama."

182. Parkes, H. B. "Nature's Diverse Laws: The Double Vision of the Elizabethans." *Sewanee Review*, 58 (1950), 402–418.

"The disharmony between two kinds of knowledge, one which interprets nature as the expression of divine reason, while the other regarded it as a battleground of amoral and destructive forces is the central theme of Elizabethan and Jacobean literature." Marlowe goes beyond most of his contemporaries in his capacity both to glorify man and to disintegrate man as his dramas expressed this central theme.

183. Peery, William. "Marlowe's Irreverent Humor—Some Open Questions." *Tulane Studies in English*, 6 (1957), 15-29.

With focus on *The Jew of Malta*, but with references to other plays as well, this writer suggests that Marlowe's humor is not merely present to "shock" audiences nor does it consist of interpolations of others, but rather that Marlowe himself was a conscious humorist, an artist who did not take everything he said in his plays as seriously as some critics would have us believe.

184. Perret, Marion D. "Theme and Structure in the Plays of Christopher Marlowe." *DAI*, 30 (1969), 288A-289A. (Yale University)

185. Peschmann, Hermann. "Christopher Marlowe, 1564-1593: 'Infinite Riches in a Little Room'." *English*, 15 (1964), 85-89.

Instead of using Marlowe's life as a basis for interpreting his works, we ought to reverse the process. The works are highly subjective and show their author's fascination with ambition. Marlowe seems to have been an agnostic, not an atheist.

186. Phillips, Barry. "Marlowe: A Revaluation." *DAI*, 29 (1969), 2681A. (University of Connecticut)

187. Pinciss, Gerald. *Christopher Marlowe*. (World Dramatists Series) New York: Frederick Ungar Publishing Co., 1975. 138 pp.

A readable and modest introductory work, but with valuable comments on Marlowe's developing skill as a dramatist, culminating in *Edward II*, where he masters "dramatic instead of lyric blank verse." Brief histories of stage productions are included by Pinciss, as well as photographs of recent Marlowe productions.

188. Poirier, Michel. *Christopher Marlowe.* London: Chatto & Windus, 1951. Reprinted, 1968. x + 216 pp.

An unabashedly romantic conception of the man and artist holds this well-wrought study together: "A man of the Renaissance, he is the incarnation of his age perhaps more than any of his fellow-countrymen. . . . His youthful works are filled to overflowing with that confidence in the power of man and in his destiny which is the chief feature of the Renaissance, that age of youth" (p. 44). Egotism and ambition reside at the core of both his life and his works—an admirer of Machiavelli's thought and an opponent of religion, although, Poirier points out, Marlowe's "atheism" in perspective was more likely deism. Poirier sees Marlowe's greatness resting ultimately on his poetry, for even his best play, *Doctor Faustus,* is not suited for the modern stage.

Chapters are Marlowe's Life, The Man and His Ideas; Apprenticeship; Tamburlaine; Doctor Faustus; Two Machiavellian Dramas; Edward II; Hero and Leander; Conclusion: Marlowe the Poet.

Reviews include Robert Fricker, *English Studies,* 34 (1953), 133–135.

189. Potter, Robert. *The English Morality Play.* London and Boston: Routledge and Kegan Paul, 1975.

Includes a trenchant discussion of Marlowe, particularly of *Doctor Faustus,* a work in which we see the dramatist has forged "out of the overlapping dramas of old certainty and new ambition, old punishment and new despair. It is built over the ruins of the old myth of a forgiving universe. It is the first, and in some ways the greatest, of the Elizabethan religious tragedies." Overall, this work is a fine survey of the subject and its implications for the major Elizabethan and Jacobean dramatists.

190. Powell, Jocelyn. "Marlowe's Spectable." *Tulane Drama Review,* 8:4 (1964), 195–210.

Action, sight, and language are integrated highly in Marlowe's plays; character and spectacle, as in the earlier morality plays, are interdependent.

191. Price, Hereward T. "Shakespeare and His Young Contemporaries." *Philological Quarterly,* 41 (1962), 37–57.

Marlowe gave ideas to his characters but not nobility or

conflict with other characters of magnitude in his plays. Each
hero embodies the dominating central idea of the play.

192. Pryor, Mary Ann. "Christopher Marlowe and the Arts of
   Persuasion." *DAI*, 27 (1966), 460A–461A. (University of
   Nebraska)

193. Rabkin, Norman and Bluestone, Max, eds. *Shakespeare's
   Contemporaries.* Englewood Cliffs, New Jersey: Prentice-
   Hall, 1961. xx + 300 pp. Reprinted and expanded, 1971.
     Reprints essays, book excerpts, and journal articles on
major plays and dramatists from Preston to Shirley. Excerpts from
studies of Marlowe include those by Paul Kocher (1946), Levin
(156), Mahood (160), and Boas (68); also essays on *Tamburlaine*
by Duthie and Gardner; essays on *Faustus* by Mizener and
Greg (1943 and 1946 respectively); and Irving Ribner on *Edward
II* (26). The revised version also includes Rothstein (483); Sanders
(207); and Waith (577)

194. Rees, Ennis. "Chapman's *Blind Beggar* and the Marlovian
   Hero." *Journal of English and Germanic Philology*, 57
   (1958), 60–63.
     Interprets Chapman's play as a satire of Marlowe's heroes,
especially *Tamburlaine;* the displays of Marlowe-like histrionics
are reasons for the popularity of Chapman's play.

195. Ribner, Irving. *The English History Play in the Age of
   Shakespeare.* 1957; rev. ed. London: Methuen & Co., 1965.
   xii + 356 pp.
     Widely regarded as a definitive treatment of the subject;
an extensive survey of the dramatic genre and of the major Renaissance philosophies of history that the plays attempt to or successfully express. Significant space is devoted to *Tamburlaine* and
its relationship to classical historiography and its theatrical impact;
also excellent pages on *Edward II.* Extensive bibliographies of
primary and secondary sources. See especially pp. 123–133 and
185–200 for extended discussions of Marlowe's plays.

196. ———. "Greene's Attack on Marlowe: Some Light on *Alphonsus* and *Selimus.*" *Studies in Philology*, 52 (1955), 162–
   171.

The attack on Marlowe in *Perimedes the Blacksmith* is not based on Greene's jealousy of Marlowe's dramatic success with 1 and 2 *Tamburlaine,* but on the politics expressed by Marlowe's hero. Both *Alphonsus* and *Selimus* show the destructive side of power that Marlowe glorifies; both emphasize the "horror" of the idea which Tamburlaine represents.

197. ———. "Marlowe and Machiavelli." *Comparative Literature,* 6 (1954), 348–356.

While the caricatures of the stage "Machiavel" in Marlowe owe much to the anti-Machiavellian literature, such as Gentillet's "Contre-Machiavel" and the stage traditions of the Vice in Tudor drama, Marlowe's knowledge of Machiavelli's actual writings seems in evidence in *Tamburlaine.*

198. ———. "Marlowe and Shakespeare." *Shakespeare Quarterly,* 15:2 (1964), 41–53. Also issued as commemorative volume, *Shakespeare 400,* James G. McManaway, ed. New York: Holt, Rinehart, & Winston, 1964. Same pagination.

Marlowe's genuine influence on Shakespeare was slight; both men reacted to the same changes and circumstances of their time oppositely; Marlowe's universe is hostile, without the ultimate sense of order upon which Shakespeare's plays seem to rely (see especially p. 51).

199. ———. "Marlowe and the Critics." *Tulane Drama Review,* 8:4 (1964), 211–224.

Surveys the state of criticism from 1597 through 1962, with emphasis on the debate over Marlowe's orthodoxy (Battenhouse [64] and Cole [90]) or his rebellious heterodoxy (Levin [156]).

200. ———. "Marlowe's 'Tragicke Glass'." In *Essays on Shakespeare and Elizabethan Drama in Honor of Hardin Craig,* pp. 91–114. Richard Hosley, editor. Columbia: University of Missouri Press, 1962.

Assesses Marlowe's contribution to English tragedy; sees Marlowe moving in the direction of Christianity in his last play (*Doctor Faustus*) though he is unwilling to embrace it outright: "we find that in his last two plays he was able to present a comprehensive view of mankind and to make some statement about the relation of good and evil in the world, as every tragic vision must. He could, however, find no real principle of order in the universe, no hope for human triumph over evil, and the only consolation he could afford to mankind was in the heroic stature of a stoic acceptance and submission to what must be" (p. 113).

201. Richmond, Velma Bourgeois. "Renaissance Sexuality and Marlowe's Women." *Ball State University Forum*, 16:4 (1975), 36–44.

Womanly virtues of humility, compassion, and acceptance of God's will represent weakness to Marlowe. His women are depicted as ineffectual and "in Marlowe's plays are usually simplified to destructive forces in men's lives. Nonetheless, the residual values of Christianity and the emerging importance of Elizabethan women at least have led Marlowe to a complex treatment of women in the *Tamburlaine* plays" (p. 44).

202. Riggs, David. *Shakespeare's Heroical Histories: Henry VI and Its Literary Tradition*. Cambridge, Massachusetts: Harvard University Press, 1971. xii + 194 pp.

Pp. 1–92 are extremely valuable in setting what Riggs contends the context of Shakespeare's dramatic accomplishment in the first tetralogy; the emphasis is on the impact of *Tamburlaine*, with the author asserting the importance of the rhetorical expression of Renaissance historiography upon the drama, and most of all on Marlowe.

Reviews include Irving Ribner, "Shakespeare's History Plays: The Romantic or Heroic View," *Medievalia et Humanistica*, NS 4 (1973), 203–210.

203. Röhrman, Hendrick. *Marlowe and Shakespeare: A Thematic Exposition of Some of Their Plays*. Arnhem: Van Loghum Slaterus, 1953.

Argues for Tamburlaine and Faustus (and three Shakespearean heroes) as forerunners of modern man. Reviews include Paul H. Kocher, *Shakespeare Quarterly*, 5 (1954), 86–88; John Russell Brown, *Modern Language Review*, 49 (1954), 112–113; and *TLS*, 27 February, 1954, p. 142.

204. Rowse, A. L. *Christopher Marlowe: His Life and Works*. New York and Evanston, Illinois: Harper & Row, 1964. xiv + 220 pp. (Universal Library Edition, Grosset & Dunlap, 1966).

A lively, informal account of the life and works giving a

flavor for Elizabethan adventurism along the way. Marlowe's early death Rowse calls the greatest individual loss to our literature. Copiously illustrated; a work for the general reader rather than scholar.

Reviews are numerous and include Terence Spencer, *The Listener*, 72 (1964):524; John Russell Brown, The *Times* (London) 6 September, 1964, p. 36; C. B. Cox, *Spectator*, 4 September, 1964, pp. 313–314; *TLS*, 3 September, 1964, p. 810; Frank Kermode, *New Statesman*, 68 (1964), 402–404; Christopher Ricks, *Observer*, 6 September, 1964, p. 24; G. B. Harrison, *The New York Times Book Review*, 24 January, 1965, p. 6; and Irving Ribner, *College English*, 27 (1965), 182–183.

205. Rozett, Martha E. T. "The Protagonist as Other in the Plays of Christopher Marlowe: A Study in the Development of Elizabethan Tragedy." *DAI*, 35 (1974), 415A. (University of Michigan)

206. Rush, Richard R. "Studies in Renaissance Concepts of Pride: Spenser and Marlowe." *DAI*, 31 (1971), 6630A. (University of California at Los Angeles)

207. Sanders, Wilbur. *The Dramatist and the Received Idea: Studies in the Plays of Marlowe and Shakespeare.* Cambridge: Cambridge University Press, 1968. xi + 390 pp.

A substantial and reasonable challenge of historicist readings of Shakespeare and Marlowe based on constructs such as "Renaissance man," or "Elizabethan world picture" or "orthodoxy." He sees *The Massacre* as largely a melodrama where the moral ambiguity may show us that Marlowe's own stance towards his subject may be "that perhaps he stands precisely nowhere" (p. 35). In *The Jew of Malta* we have both sentimentality and brutality, where the ideas promulgated by Machiavel in the Prologue are "ideological constructs" where "the world in which the ideas are held is not a human one, but a diagrammatic representation of that world" (p. 59). Like *Richard III*, Marlowe's play confronts "that new social and political world which is presided over by the tutelary genius of Machiavelli" (p. 60). *Edward II's* grimness is a function of inhumanity; Marlowe does not objectively report the action; rather "The equable tone in which Marlowe enunciates his horrors, the strange bareness of diction, is not the result of a classical restraint, or of some new discipline of art. The play is amoral, not by intention, but by default" (p. 142). *Doctor Faustus* has a sporadic grasp of reality but "its reach is tremendous. We are watching a man, I suggest, locked in a death embrace with the agonising God he can neither reject nor love. It is the final consummation of the Puritan imagination" (p. 235).

In this probing and often infuriating book, Sanders raises some real and tough questions about our methodologies in approaching Marlowe and Shakespeare both. The book has been reviewed variously. J. L. Styan, *Modern Language Quarterly*, 29 (1968), 483-486; *TLS*, 4 July, 1968, p. 706; Kenneth Muir, *Review of English Studies*, 20 (1969), 211-213; Douglas Cole, *Modern Philology*, 67 (1969), 376-379; Michael Manheim, *Hartford Studies in Literature*, 2 (1969), 85-91; Marco Mincoff, *English Studies*, 51 (1969), 157-160; Roy W. Battenhouse, *Shakespeare Studies*, 5 (1969), 357-367; Alfred Harbage, *Renaissance Quarterly*, 22 (1969), 63-65.

208. Savas, Minas. "The Making and Unmaking of Three Marlovian Heroes." *DAI*, 32 (1972), 4579A. (University of California, Santa Barbara)

209. Seaton, Ethel. "Marlowe's Light Reading." In *Elizabethan and Jacobean Studies presented to F. P. Wilson in Honor of His Seventieth Birthday*, pp. 17-35. Herbert Davis and Helen Gardner, eds. Oxford: Clarendon Press, 1960.
   "The romances are the culture bed in which the seeds of Marlowe's young imagination germinated. It is no wonder that, crossed with classical and oriental stocks, the full flowering is exotic, flamboyant, brilliant in colour and light" (p. 35). Shows Marlowe's reading of romance literature was probably extensive.

210. Sellin, Paul R. "The Hidden God: Reformation Awe in Renaissance Literature." In *The Darker Vision of the Renaissance: Beyond the Fields of Reason*, pp. 147-196. (U.C.L.A. Center for Medieval and Renaissance Contributions, No. 6) Robert S. Kinsman, editor. Berkeley and Los Angeles: University of California Press, 1974.
   Contains references to Marlowe's works.

211. Seyler, Dorothy U. "The Critical Reputation of Christopher Marlowe. 1800–1899." *DAI*, 30 (1970), 3435A–3436A. (State University of New York at Albany)

212. Shand, George B. "Stage Techniques in the Plays of Christopher Marlowe." *DAI*, 32 (1971), 400a. (University of Toronto)

213. Shield H. A. "Charles Sledd, Spymaster." *Notes and Queris*, NS 7 (1960), 47–48.
Describes career of this suborner of false-witness who was an associate of Ingram Frizer, Marlowe's alleged murderer.

214. ———. "The Death of Marlowe." *Notes and Queries*, NS 4 (1957), 101–103.
Suggests a double connection in Marlowe's role as one of Walsingham's agents.

215. Sims, James H. *Dramatic Uses of Biblical Allusion in Marlowe and Shakespeare.* (University of Florida Monographs in the Humanities, No. 24) Gainesville: University of Florida Press, 1966. iii + 82 pp.
Identifies three principal types of Biblical allusion in Marlowe that invert original Scriptural meanings; especially in *The Jew of Malta* and *Doctor Faustus.*

216. Speaight, Robert. "Marlowe: The Forerunner." *Review of English Literature*, 7:4 (1966), 26–41.
Marlowe's skill greatest as a narrative poet; he is less the forerunner of Shakespeare than of Milton.

217. Sprott, S. E. "Drury and Marlowe." *TLS*, 2 August, 1974, p. 840.
Reprints letter of one Thomas Drury dated 1 August, 1593 to Anthony Bacon, referring allegedly to Richard Baines and to the "atheist lecture," indicating that Drury played a part in the affair of that previous spring involving the death of Marlowe.

218. Steane, J. B. *Marlowe: A Critical Study.* Cambridge: University Press, 1964. viii + 383 pp.
Marlowe's life and works scrutinized from the "reactionary" point of view (p. vi) by Steane, whose primary interest is

Marlowe's poetry. For Steane, Marlowe is restless and contradictory in both his life and work; chapters are devoted to all of the plays in order of composition; then to translations and to *Hero and Leander*, with a concluding chapter excoriating those who have approached Marlowe's work with a conception already invented about the man. Steane writes that the most striking thing about reading Marlowe's works carefully is that "Individuality is preserved: there is no mistaking Marlowe's voice in any of his works" (p. 346).

Reviews include C. B. Cox (entry 92); *TLS*, 23 April, 1964, p. 338; L. Lerner, *Listener*, 71 (1964), 686; Roy W. Battenhouse, *Modern Language Quarterly*, 25 (1964), 496–497; John D. Jump, *Critical Quarterly*, 6 (1964), 380–381; Robert Kimbrough, *Journal of English and Germanic Philology*, 63 (1965), 773–775; R. Proudfoot, *Durham University Journal*, 26 (1965), 61–62; Michel Poirier, *Études Anglaises*, 19 (1965), 69–70; G. R. Hibbard, *Notes and Queries*, NS 12 (1965), 116–117; Douglas Cole, *Modern Philology*, 63 (1965), 154–157; Clifford Leech, *Shakespeare Studies*, 1 (1965), 337–339.

219. Stroup, Thomas B. *Microcosmos: The Shape of the Elizabethan Play.* Lexington: University of Kentucky Press, 1965. xi + 235 pp.

Contains comments of a general nature regarding Marlowe's plays on the action of characters set against the larger macrocosm kingdom, world, or universe; pageantry and procession; the representation of the different strata of society in the worlds of the plays.

220. ———. "Ritual in Marlowe's Plays." *Comparative Drama*, 7 (1973), 198–221.

Identifies sixty "formal or ceremonial processions" in the plays and explains their dramatic uses: presentation of the crown (*Dido*); triumphal conqueror (*1T*); royal power and slate (*Edward II*); funeral procession (*2T*); disgrace (*The Jew of Malta*); international incident (*Massacre*); burlesque and satire (*Doctor Faustus*); he also identifies rituals and ceremonies in the plays. Stroup believes these many processionals often ironically undermine the actions of the characters.

221. Summers, Claude J. *Christopher Marlowe and the Politics of Power.* (Elizabethan and Renaissance Studies, No. 22)

Editor: James Hogg. Salzburg: Institut fur Englische Sprache und Literatur, 1974. vi + 203 pp.

A fresh consideration of political ideas in all the plays, the author explains, "because all of Marlowe's dramas, to a greater or lesser extent, are concerned with questions of power and choices between political systems" (p. iii). He devotes a chapter to Tudor political thought before analyzing the plays. He concludes that Marlowe's politics are as diverse as his dramas; in one play, *Tamburlaine*, he presents a romanticized vision of the man of *virtu*, while in another, he shows with bitterness a world in which such principles operate universally (*The Jew of Malta*). Marlowe uses politics for dramatic effect; "What is certain, however, is that Machiavellianism interested him throughout his career and that he explored the subject from a variety of aspects and used it as a dramatic tool" (p. 198). In elucidating the political implications of Marlowe's plays, often very tellingly, Summers hopes to show how these enrich our awareness of Marlowe's artistic accomplishment.

222. Talbert, Ernest W. *Elizabethan Drama and Shakespeare's Early Plays: An Essay in Historical Criticism.* Chapel Hill: University of North Carolina Press, 1963. v + 410 pp.

Deals with Shakespeare's early plays in light of contemporary drama, especially, Lyly, Marlowe, Greene, and Kyd. Identifies common elements involving character types and structures of plot and action. Extensive reference to Marlowe throughout. In *The Massacre at Paris* (pp. 87–90), Marlowe is seen working with conventional attitudes about the Machiavel, but the ideas which constitute what makes a good or bad ruler are essentially medieval; *Edward II* possesses a basic structural movement of "errors or viciousness before the fall from power, pity after it" (p. 95; see pp. 95–110); in *Tamburlaine* (pp. 110–121) Marlowe uses the repetitive pattern of the heroic drama to greater advantage than before.

223. Thurston, Gavin. "Christopher Marlowe's Death." *Contemporary Review*, 205 (1964), 156–159; 193–200.

A barrister's examination of information known about Marlowe's death includes a biography and an inquest proper which acquits Frizer of assassination. "Marlowe's nature was such that a violent end was inevitable in a violent age. His acrid tongue was calculated to provoke such an incident as killed him. There seems no need to look behind it for a devious political intrigue" (p. 200).

224. Tomilson, T. B. *A Study of Elizabethan and Jacobean Tragedy.* Cambridge: Cambridge University Press, 1964. viii + 293 pp.

Pp. 48–94 concerned largely with Marlowe (and with Kyd); Tomilson sees *Tamburlaine* largely as a poetic and dramatic failure, whereas in *Faustus* "it is still a matter of fairly simple concepts—like energetic humanism and conservative Christianity—'being controlled.' But in this play, unlike *Tamburlaine*, the element of control inheres in the intelligence which juxtaposes the twin values, not merely in verse structure as such" (p. 71).

225. Turner, Robert Y. "Pathos and the *Gorboduc* Tradition, 1560–1590." *Huntington Library Quarterly,* 25 (1962), 97–120.

Shows how classical lament was incorporated into drama, culminating at the close of the period discussed with *The Spanish Tragedy* and *Dido, Queen of Carthage.*

226. Urry, William. "Marlowe and Canterbury." *TLS,* 13 February, 1964, p. 136.

Recounts Marlowe's two adult visits to Canterbury, 1585 and 1592; traces fortunes of Marlowe's relatives and shows that the poet's father, John, "was a character all in his own right."

227. Waith, Eugene M. *The Herculean Hero in Marlowe, Chapman, Shakespeare, and Dryden.* New York: Columbia University Press; London: Chatto & Windus, 1962. 224 pp.

An impressive account of the development of the figure of Herculean hero from antiquity to the Renaissance; the section on Marlowe (pp. 60–87) deals almost exclusively with Tamburlaine as a paradigm of the Herculean hero in drama.

Reviews include Ernest Shanzer, *Modern Language Review,* 59 (1962), 263–264; C. Rees, *Journal of English and Germanic Philology,* 63 (1964), 491–497; I. Ribner, *Criticism,* 5:183–185; G. K. Hunter, *Durham University Journal,* 24 (1962), 152–153; Michel Poirier, *Études Anglaises,* 16 (1963), 181–182; Horst Oppel, *Anglia,* 88:483–487; Kenneth Muir, *Listener,* 67:1039–1040.

228. ———. *Ideas of Greatness: Heroic Drama in England.* London: Routledge & Kegan Paul, 1971. xii + 292 pp.

Traces the romantic origins of heroic drama in detail; his cogent analysis of *Tamburlaine* (pp. 35–123) stresses Marlowe's translation of romantic virtues of heroism into drama. Review in *TLS*, 29 October, 1971, p. 1361.

229. Weil, Judith E. R. *Christopher Marlowe: Merlin's Prophet.* Cambridge: Cambridge University Press, 1977. vii + 219 pp.

Weil's study challenges both the ironic and romantic critics of Marlowe; her essential argument "is that Marlowe mocks his heroes in a remarkably subtle fashion" (p. 2). Marlowe *is* an ironic artist, she claims, but at the expense of his heroes, and his manipulation of audience sympathies is often based on the dramatist's respect, rather than opprobrium, for its collective intelligence. Marlowe's "prophetic" style is based upon his use of allusions—often inverted or half-quoted; soliloquies ("It is as if the speaker seizes upon the advantages of soliloquy to commend himself and his desires," p. 14); and spectable. There is much to commend in individual readings of speeches and actions in the plays throughout this brief study, but the reader may question how one critic has finally happened upon the super-subtle ironic meanings after so many generations of readers and audiences since Marlowe's day have failed to turn these up.

Reviews include Roma Gill, *TLS*, 12 May, 1978, p. 525.

230. ———. "Expository Techniques in Marlowe's Plays." *DAI*, 32 (1972), 4582A–4583A. (Stanford)

231. Welsh, Robert Ford. "The Printing of Early Editions of Marlowe's Plays: *Tamburlaine* (1590); *The Massacre at Paris* (1592?); *Edward II* (1594); *Dido* (1594); *Doctor Faustus* (1604, 1616); *The Jew of Malta* (1633)." *DAI*, 25 (1964), 2968–2929. (Duke University)

An extended essay in analytical bibliography designed to identify printers and dates of publication where not known or confirmed; the order of formes; the identification of compositors and their respective shares. Very well-regarded work by eminent bibliographer (see entry 8).

231a. Wernham, R. B. "Christopher Marlowe at Flushing in 1592." *English Historical Review*, 91 (1976), 344–45.

Points out that the informer Baines, in addition to the accusations leveled at Marlowe in his famous "Note", had earlier accused him of counterfeiting.

232. Wham, Benjamin. "Marlowe's Mighty Line: Was Marlowe Murdered at Twenty-Nine?" *American Bar Association Journal*, 46 (1960), 509–513.

No, he wasn't. Spirited abroad, he wrote Shakespeare's plays. Wham "proves" his case by showing dozens of examples where the two authors (who are in his reality one man, Marlowe) compose similar lines of verse or evoke similar images or make similar allusions.

233. Wickham, Glynne. "*Exeunt to the Cave:* Notes on the Staging of Marlowe's Plays." *Tulane Drama Review*, 8:4 (1964), 184–194.

The bleakness of Marlowe's vision is mitigated onstage by color and movement—swift scene changes move us from one great speech to the next; Marlowe's stage was not elaborately machined; it was an "emblematic stage simple enough to allow swift moving action."

234. ———. *Shakespeare's Dramatic Heritage.* London: Routledge & Kegan Paul, 1969.

Reprints *TDR* essay (entry 233), pp. 121–131.

235. Williams, David Rhys. *Shakespeare, Thy Name Is Marlowe.* New York: Philosopher's Library, 1966.

Protected by Thomas Walsingham, Marlowe wrote Shakespeare. Someone else was killed at Deptford.

236. Williamson, Hugh Ross. *Kind Kit: An Informal Biography of Christopher Marlowe.* London: Michael Joseph, 1972. 269 pp.

Begins with the ambiguous circumstances surrounding Marlowe's death and leaves the questions of Marlowe's "various lives" hanging over the whole account. Dialogue is invented throughout to give this lively speculation greater verisimilitude. A postscript on Marlowe and Shakespeare would seem to put to rest the idea that they were one in the same. Readable and believable; Marlowe as a "very-important-person" in his own time.

237. Wilson, Frank Percy. *Marlowe and the Early Shakespeare.*
Being the Clark Lectures presented at Trinity College,
Cambridge, 1951. Oxford: Clarendon Press, 1953. iv + 144
pp.

Still a worthy and influential introduction to the subject,
though textual theories, in part, are outdated. Wilson sees Marlowe as the apologist for the renaissance man who "must have
courage *and* brains, haughtiness of heart *and* a reaching and
imaginative mind. And to Marlowe . . . Tamburlaine was the su-
preme type of such a man" (p. 24). Wilson sees Marlowe celebrating these profound energies of his time in *Tamburlaine,* leaving
moral choice to the audience; *The Jew of Malta* Wilson tries to
argue away with textual disintegration theories (unconvincingly);
he maintains a similar position about *Faustus,* but claims that
Marlowe's involvement with his subject is profound in any case
(p. 77). *Edward II* is his one full study of kingship (p. 102) and its
abdication scene contains a pathos which clearly Shakespeare re-
membered when writing *Richard II.* The final chapter discusses
the relationship between the two dramatists; he finds ambiguity
in Marlowe and not in Shakespeare, just as he finds no orthodox
system or order in the former which is found in the latter. Believing *Hero and Leander* and *Faustus* are products of Marlowe's last
year, Wilson concludes that Shakespeare's sonnet 86, if dated
early, refers to Marlowe as the rival poet.

Reviews include E. M. W. Tillyard, *Modern Language
Review,* 49:223–224; T. M. Parrott, *Shakespeare Quarterly,* 5
(1954), 179–186; Michel Poirier, *Études Anglaises,* 7 (1954), 319;
Peter Ure, *Review of English Studies,* 5 (1954), 71–73; Hallet
Smith, *Yale Review,* 48:121–125; *University of Toronto Quarterly,*
24:102–105; *TLS,* 17 April, 1953, p. 24.

238. Wilson, John Delane. "Some Uses of Physiognomy in the
Plays of Shakespeare, Jonson, Marlowe, and Dekker." *DAI,*
26 (1966), 4642. (Michigan State University)

239. Wraight, A. D. *In Search of Christopher Marlowe: A Picto-
rial Biography.* Photography by Virginia F. Stern. London:
MacDonald, 1964.

A very attractive popular biography with copious illus-
trations. Reviews include M. Seymour Smith, *Spectator,* 6 August 1965, p. 182; *TLS,* 26 August, 1964, p. 736; F. N. Jones,

Library Journal, 90 (1964), 4082–4084; B. Grebanier, *Saturday Review*, 25 December, 1965, pp. 33–34.

240. Zimansky, Curt A. "Comment on Marlowe." *TLS*, 6 April, 1956, p. 207. Response to entry 52.

241. Zucker, David H. "Stage and Image in the Plays of Christopher Marlowe." *DAI*, 29 (1969), 4030A–4031A. (Syracuse University)

242. ————. *Stage and Image in the Plays of Christopher Marlowe*. (Elizabethan and Renaissance Studies, No. 7) James Hogg, editor. Salzburg: Institut fur Englische Sprache and Literatur, 1972. 188 pp.
     A reassessment of theatrical metaphor and stagecraft in Marlowe, showing his skills as a writer for the stage.

3. POEMS AND TRANSLATIONS

243. Adamson, Jane. "Marlowe, *Hero and Leander,* and the Art
of Leaping in Poetry." *The Critical Review,* 17 (1974),
59–81.
      The emphasis in Marlowe's poem is on flux and change.
The image of humanity in the poem is rendered in terms of
character types rather than integral personalities, so that human
relationships are seen as the struggle for dominance by one type
over others.

244. Baldwin, T. W. "Marlowe's Musaeus." *Journal of English
and Germanic Philology,* 54 (1955), 478–485.
      Argues that Marlowe used the Greek original for *Hero
and Leander.*

245. Banerjee, Chinmoy. "*Hero and Leander* as Erotic Comedy."
Journal of Narrative Technique, 3 (1973), 40–52.
      Comic action operates at two levels in Marlowe's poem;
first, in the self-conscious narrator who is a naïve moralist and
whose absurd conceits are framed in the false assumption that his
audience is as naïve as he; second, the ironic relation between
the narrative action and the problem of the lover's separation. No
matter how immense the obstacles thwarting them are, they sur-
mount barriers with relative ease, further undercutting the
"poet's tale" and implied moral.

246. Bowers, Fredson. "The Early Editions of Marlowe's
Elegies." *Studies in Bibliography,* 25 (1972), 149–172.
      Determines order of the first two editions that contain only
a selection of elegies; the third edition, the first "complete" one,
took the first printed edition as its copy text for previously published poems, while others were based on manuscript versions.
The fourth and fifth editions are in turn based on the third.

247. Cantelupe, Eugene B. "*Hero and Leander*, Marlowe's
Tragicomedy of Love." *College English*, 24 (1963), 295–298.
 Marlowe's plays are largely tragic, but his great poem is a
glorious mixture of tragedy and high comedy. Its comical rhetoric
and exuberant poetry, the naïvety of the lovers, go hand in hand
with their passionate desire for each other that verges "on comic
folly and tragic madness" (p. 298).

248. Collins, S. Ann. "Sundrie Shapes, Committing Headie
Ryots, Incest, Rapes: Functions of Myth in Determining
Narrative in Marlowe's *Hero and Leander*." *Mosaic*, 4:1
(1970), 107–122.
 Studies digressions in the poem to show that "Epic sublim-
ity is constantly undermined, optimism deflated, and romanticism
pierced at its swelling crest each time by cynicism." Marlowe's
work suggests that Love is "unquiet, predatory, and glorious,"
the immersion of the "self in a destructive element."

249. Cubeta, Paul M. "Marlowe's Poet in *Hero and Leander*."
College English, 26 (1965), 500–505.
 The narrator, with his bawdiness and hyperbole, is at odds
with the high seriousness of the "poet," thus showing Marlowe's
satiric intent.

250. Eden, John M. "Hero and Belinda." *Notes and Queries*, NS
4 (1957), 12–13.
 Notes parallels between Pope's heroine and Marlowe's.

250a. Farkas, David Kalman. "Problems of Interpretation in Marlowe's *Hero and Leander*. " *DAI*, 37 (1977), 6494 A.

251. Fraser, Russell A. "The Art of *Hero and Leander*." *Journal
of English and Germanic Philology*, 57 (1958), 743–754.
 Fraser defends Marlowe's sense of humor. The fantastical
conceits, the hyperbole, the unintentional bawdry are conscious
devices used by Marlowe to undermine the pretensions of
Musaeus' original.

252. Fredin, Lowell E. "The Variant Muse: A Study of *Hero and
Leander* and Elizabethan Love Narrative." *DAI*, 32 (1972),
5180A–5181A. (University of Ohio)

253. Gill, Roma and Robert Krueger. "The Early Editions of
   Marlowe's *Elegies* and Davies' *Epigrams:* Sequence and Authority." *Library,* 26 (1971), 242-249.
   Mason's edition is the third, following upon Bindley and
Isham. For Marlowe's poems Mason's edition is important because he must have had a new manuscript copy to work with
throughout.

254. Gill, Roma. "Marlowe, Lucan, and Sulpitius." *Review
   of English Studies,* 49 (1973), 401-413.
   Marlowe's translation of the *Pharsalia* is the best of its
time (superior to versions by Arthur Georges and Thomas May)
because he relies on Sulpitius' Commentary and Text of Lucan.
Marlowe has appropriated both examples and errors not found in
Lucan's original but in Sulpitius; overall, these borrowings and
adaptations greatly enliven Marlowe's version.

255. ———. "Snake Leape by Verse." In *Christopher Marlowe,* pp. 133-150. Brian Morris, ed. (See entry 170.)
   An investigation of the techniques Marlowe used and the
verbal habits he followed in translating Ovid. Gill finds him most
creative and free as a translator when most involved with the
individual Latin poems, most literal and ordinary when not.

256. Halio, Jay L. "Perfection and Elizabethan Ideas of Conception." *English Language Notes,* 1 (1964), 179-182.
   Includes a reference to *Hero and Leander* (I, 265-268),
pointing out Marlowe's dual intent: the lines are bawdy, but also
representative of the Aristotelian notion that women can attain
their perfection only through men.

257. Hardin, Richard F. "Michael Drayton and the Ovidian Tra-
   dition." *DAI,* 27 (1967), 3428A. (University of Texas at
   Austin)
   With some reference to *Hero and Leander.*

258. Jacobsen, Eric. *Translation: A Traditional Craft: An Introductory Sketch with a Study of Marlowe's Elegies.* Copenha-
   gen, 1958.
   A study of habits and methods of translation as an art in

the English Renaissance, with close attention to the methods of Marlowe in his translations from Ovid's *Amores*. Reviews include M. Colker, *Spectator*, 34 (1959), 286–287.

259. Jahn, Gerald D. "The Elizabethan Epyllion: Its Art and Narrative Conventions." *DAI*, 33 (1972), 2331A. (University of Indiana)
  Includes discussion of *Hero and Leander*.

260. Keach, William. "Marlowe's Hero as 'Venus' Nun'." *English Literary Renaissance*, 2 (1972), 207–220.
  The phrase appearing in the first sestiad, line 45, about Hero, suggests the basis of Marlowe's ironic presentation of her. Keach sees Marlowe extending implications found in Musaeus, namely, the contradictory demands placed on Hero as being Venus' nun (*ergo* chaste) and being servant to the goddess of love and sexuality. Hero is seen as passionate and intelligent; the consummation of the sexual act brings her to a recognition of her true state in terms of shame, vulnerability, and insincerity—risks in human love relationships.

261. Kŏstic, Veselin. "Marlowe's *Hero and Leander* and Chapman's *Continuation*." In *Renaissance and Modern Essays Presented to Vivian de Sola Pinto in Celebration of His Seventieth Birthday*, pp. 25–34. G. A. Panichas and Allan Rodway, eds. London: Routledge & Kegan Paul, 1966.
  An overview of the possible continuity, unity, and differences in the two portions of the completed poem.

262. Leech, Clifford. "'Venus and the Nun': Portraits of Women in Love in Shakespeare and Marlowe." *Studies in English Literature*, 5 (1965), 247–268.
  A valuable comparative study of *Hero and Leander* and *Venus and Adonis* especially. Marlowe's Venus is representative of the destructive power of love, whereas Shakespeare's Venus is comical. Marlowe's depicture of the gods makes fun of the "supernatural order men once fashioned for themselves" to explain their behavior. Leech believes this position is close to Marlowe's view of supernatural order in the plays, too. He says, however, that despite their obvious frailties, Marlowe treats men and women in love with affection, as does Shakespeare.

263. Leiter, Louis H. "Deification through Love: Marlowe's 'The Passionate Shepherd to His Love'." *College English*, 27 (1966), 444–449.

An explication of Marlowe's lyric that shows how the shepherdness is demonstrably transformed into the goddess Flora.

264. Lewis, C. S. "Hero and Leander." *Proceedings of the British Academy*, 38 (1952), 23–38. Reprinted in *Elizabethan Poetry: Modern Essays in Criticism*. Paul Alpers, ed. Oxford and New York: Oxford University Press, 1967, pp. 235–250.

Lewis contends that the whole poem is remarkable, that Marlowe and Chapman contributed to the story and to the work what the other poet could not. Marlowe writes "within erotic frenzy" and shows not what lust is but instead what lust thinks it sees. Marlowe's treatment is exuberant because of its masculine metre; his account of the lovers lacks tenderness but its final impression is that of "pathos." For Lewis, Marlowe's two sestiads possess a purity of form, color, and intention.

265. Long, Mike. "An Elizabethan 'Structure of Feeling'." *Cambridge Review*, 89 (1966), 58–61.

Marlowe's portion of *Hero and Leander* is light, humanistic, and puts the reader in touch with the theme of celebrating sensual man and nature. Chapman's portion, based on neo-Platonic concepts, makes the poem as a whole an excellent example of divergent strands in Renaissance culture.

266. McNeal, Thomas H. "The Names 'Hero and 'Don John' in *Much Ado*." *Notes and Queries*, 198 (1953), 382.

Hero comes from Marlowe's poem. Proof suggested is that Jonson alludes to Marlowe's poem at the same time of *Much Ado*, when he was closely associated with Shakespeare.

267. Marsh, T. N. "Marlowe's *Hero and Leander*, I, 45–50." *Explicator*, 21 (1963), Item 30.

Hyperbolic praise of Hero is really an "explanation of Night rather than Negroes."

268. Maxwell, J. C. "*Hero and Leander* and *Love's Labour's Lost*." *Notes and Queries*, 198 (1953), 334–335.

Suggests a later date for the Shakespeare comedy on the strength of an echo in IV.iii,262–264 to *Hero and Leander*, I, 49–50: "there seems no difficulty in believing that the manuscript for *Hero and Leander* was accessible to Shakespeare at any time from 1593."

269. Miller, Paul W. "The Elizabethan Minor Epic." *Studies in Philology*, 55 (1958), 31–38.
     Suggests the epyllion is the proper context to interpret *Hero and Leander*, where digression from the main narrative is usually the most important element of structure, and its content often as arresting as the main tale. In digressing on a disproportionately greater scale than in classical *epyllia*, Marlowe obliterates our "moral reaction" to Hero and Leander's passion. Accordingly, he also amplifies the power of their love. The story of Mercury and the Maid in effect make Hero and Leander into representative human lovers.

270. ———. "A Function of Myth in Marlowe's *Hero and Leander*." *Studies in Philology*, 50 (1953), 158–167.
     Hero and Leander are deservedly punished for offenses against the gods.

271. ———. "The Problem of Justice in Marlowe's *Hero and Leander*." *Notes and Queries*, NS 4 (1957), 163–164.
     Under the safety of a mythological veil, Marlowe questions the orthodox Christian concept of a just God.

272. Mills, John. "The Courtship Ritual of *Hero and Leander*." *English Literary Renaissance*, 2 (1972), 298–306.
     Maintains that the lovers are controlled by forces which they cannot comprehend or understand, which prevents them from controlling their lives. Leander makes the pretense of understanding and "assumes the male role" to explain things to Hero, but he does not himself truly realize his motivations. Their "game" is physical, no matter how they delude themselves and "'polite readers' that their activities are spiritual."

273. Morris, Brian. "Comic Method in *Hero and Leander*." In *Christopher Marlowe*, pp. 113–132. Brian Morris, ed. (See entry 170.)

Following Clifford Leech, who sees the poem as a great comic masterpiece, Morris concludes: "Young love is absurd. It may seem that Marlowe's theme represents a rather cheap discovery about the human condition by one who was accustomed to explore humanity and its sufferings more deeply. The absurdity is exposed, mercilessly, right through the poem, in different ways and at varying levels. But it is not exploited. A trenchant inquiry would direct the poem inexorably towards tragedy, and, as I have tried to show, the dominant tone is comic. The central figure is the suave, detached narrator, who asserts an unshakeable comic control over narrative, allusion, and language alike. Marlowe's bias is increasingly towards full burlesque, and away from the impending tragic end of the story. Perhaps that is why he never finished it" (p. 131).

274. Morris, Harry. "Marlowe's Poetry." *Tulane Drama Review*, 8:4 (1964), 134–154.

A study of the quality of the Marlovian line, especially in the plays; Morris says Marlowe's poetry moves from Spenserian sweetness to dramatic fury. *The Jew of Malta* introduces "mature English accents, idioms, and cadences" to speech; *Edward II* subdues rhetoric. *Doctor Faustus* is Marlowe's poetic crown, bearing the glow of the earlier dramas with greater subtlety of color and tone.

275. Neuse, Richard. "Atheism and Some Functions of Myth in Marlowe's *Hero and Leander*." *Modern Language Quarterly*, 31 (1970), 424–439.

Despite surface humor, Marlowe's narrator, by his pose and his key descriptions in The Temple of Venus and the Mercury-Destiny episodes, shows man's need to sustain his own tentative, volatile, and unsure place in the cosmos with myth.

276. Nosworthy, J. M. "Marlowe's Ovid and Davies' *Epigrams:* A Postscript." *Review of English Studies*, 15 (1964), 397–398. [See *RES*, 4 (1953), 260–261.]

Reasserts 1595 date for publication of the first octavo edition of Marlowe's translation of Ovid.

276a. Ogoshi, Kazuzu. "Hero to Leander: Hyoshaku." *Eigo Seinen (The Rising Generation)*, 123, (1977), 2–5, 55–58,

114–117, 158–161, 212–215, 257–260, 301–304, 364–368, 404–407.
Commentary on Marlowe's poem.

277. Rosen, Charles. "The Progression of Atheism in Marlowe's Poetry." *Erasmus Review,* 1 (1971), 83–93.

278. Segal, Eric. "*Hero and Leander:* Gongora and Marlowe." *Comparative Literature,* 15 (1963), 338–356.
Both writers radically alter the story from Musaeus. Both exhibit an individualistic style with a cynical perspective on the romance. Marlowe's major stylistic alteration is hyperbole.

279. Sheidley, William E. "The Seduction of the Reader in Marlowe's *Hero and Leander.*" *Concerning Poetry,* 3:1 (1970), 50–56.
Readers are voyeurs in Marlowe's sensuous poem and must ultimately laugh at themselves in their titillation as they do at the exaggerated passions of the lovers in the story.

280. Smith, Hallet. *Elizabethan Poetry: A Study in Conventions, Meaning, and Expression.* Cambridge: Harvard University Press, 1952. Especially Chapter II, "Ovidian Poetry: The Growth and Adaptation of Forms," pp. 64–130.
Distinguishes two primary traditions in Elizabethan Ovidian poems: the moral-didactic tradition and that of entertainment. Marlowe's *Hero and Leander* exhibits the best characteristics of the second tradition. All elements of the poem, including characterization, are subordinate to "the standard and recognized pattern of mythological lore," compressed so ingeniously as to make the "speed of the poem . . . its essential characteristic." Smith's chapter—indeed the whole work—makes good introductory reading on the subject.

281. Smith, John T. "The Complex Vision: A Study of Christopher Marlowe's Non-Dramatic Poetry." *DAI,* 34 (1973), 740A–741A. (University of Illinois)

282. Staton, Walter F. "The Influence of Thomas Watson on Elizabethan Ovidian Poetry." *Studies in the Renaissance* (1959), 243–250.

Though Marlowe was a close friend of Watson, the author here finds that *Hero and Leander* betrays no debt to Watson.

283. Sternfeld, Frederick W. and Mary Chan. "'Come Live with Me and Be My Love." *Comparative Literature*, 22 (1970), 173–187.
Asserts and documents the popularity of Marlowe's lyric in his own time and immediately after his death. (See, too, Sternfeld's analysis of the poem in *The Hidden Harmony: Essays in Honor of Philip Wheelwright* [1966], pp. 173–192).

284. Taylor, A. B. "Britomart and the Mermaids: A Note on Marlowe and Spenser." *Notes and Queries*, NS 18 (1971), 224–225.
Hero and Leander (I, 161–164) and *The Faerie Queene*, III.4, stanzas 18 and 22.

285. ———. "A Note on Marlowe's *Hero and Leander*." *Notes and Queries*, Ns 16 (1969), 20–21.
Points out Marlowe's debt to *The Pleasant Fable of Hermaphroditis and Salamacis*, by T[homas?] Peend, published in 1565.

286. Turner, Myron. "Pastoral and Hermaphrodite: A Study of Naturalism in Marlowe's *Hero and Leander*." *Texas Studies in Literature and Language*, 17 (1975), 397–414.
Shows that the portrait of Leander is essentially serious, and that Marlowe depicts a universe in which "the tragedies of man's fate are enacted amidst the opulence and sensual beauty" of a careless natural environment. Homosexuality and hermaphroditism symbolize a universe lacking moral order; this is countered by the poet through the pastoral celebration of the erotic encounters where Hero's shame (*cf.*esp. II, 263–334) is seen in the larger context of man's fall from innocence.

287. Tyson, Mary Hanna. "Marlowe, Shakespeare, and the Ovidian Narrative Tradition." *DAI*, 27 (1966), 752A–753A. (University of California, Berkeley)

288. Walsh, William P. "Sexual Discovery and Renaissance Morality in Marlowe's *Hero and Leander*." *Studies in English Literature*, 12 (1972), 33–54.

The lovers violate Renaissance concepts of the natural beauty in procreation in their pursuit of sex which, though condemned, is treated with humorous sympathy by Marlowe.

289. Williams, Gordon I. "Acting and Suffering in *Hero and Leander.*" *Trivium*, 8 (1973), 11–26.

The poem is full of ambiguities and opposites that it seeks to reconcile. The hermaphroditic strain, as well as the conflict between chastity and licentiousness, embraces Renaissance traditions found in Neo-Platonism and Orphic theology. Both Marlowe and Chapman focus on psychological concerns that through the central characters demonstrate the paradoxes of love.

290. Williams, Martin T. "The Temptations in Marlowe's *Hero and Leander.*" *Modern Language Quarterly*, 16 (1955), 226–231.

Neptune's temptation of Leander is an episode which gives the poem greater depth.

291. Woods, Susanne. "'The Passionate Shepherd' and 'The Nimphs Reply': A Study in Transmission." *Huntington Library Quarterly*, 34 (1970), 25–33.

Shows that the poems may have been transmitted as songs, for early printed versions do not appear based on manuscript copies in possession of the Huntington Library.

292. Zocca, Louis R. *Elizabethan Narrative Poetry.* New Brunswick, N.J.: Rutgers Univ. Press, 1950. Reprinted New York: Octagon Books, 1970. See esp. Chapter XIX. "Marlowe and His Imitators," pp. 232–247.

Recounts a litany of *Hero and Leander's* flaws stemming from its incomplete state—lack of transition, unity of conception, anachronism, "mingling of the serious and mocking"—but believes these are compensated for by Marlowe's "characteristic fervor, his torrential emotion which sweeps everything before it." These stem from the poet's "self identification" with the mythology.

4. *DIDO, QUEEN OF CARTHAGE*

293. Allen, Don Cameron. "Marlowe's *Dido* and the Tradition." In *Essays on Shakespeare and Elizabethan Drama in Honor of Hardin Craig*, pp. 55–68. Richard Hosley, ed. Columbia, Missouri: University of Missouri Press, 1962.

Compares *Dido* by Marlowe to treatments of the story of Dido and Aeneas in Continental Renaissance dramas by Cinthio, Dolce, and Jodelle, concluding that Marlowe "votes with his predecessors who held the Trojan guilty" of deserting his love, and that the divine figures in Marlowe's tragedy only emphasize his ironic and skeptical attitude "towards those who think that there is a divinity that shapes our ends."

294. Brashear, Marion G. "Marlowe's Tragedy of Dido." *DAI*, 33 (1973), 3574A–3575A. (University of Washington)

295. Brodwin, Leonora Leet. *Elizabethan Love Tragedy, 1587–1625*. New York: New York University Press, London: University of London Press, 1971. xii + 404 pp.

See "Tragedies of Worldly Love," pp. 183–191, for a discussion of Marlowe's *Dido*. Brodwin sees Dido's tragic conflict as that between love for Aeneas and sovereignty, where the preservation of the latter destroys the former and where, paradoxically, "the destruction of her love . . . deprives this preservation of meaning." Aeneas is Marlowe's "Renaissance aspiring man" who, though tempted by love, soon reveals that "Its impact on his soul is slight."

296. Cope, Jackson I. "Marlowe's *Dido* and the Titillating Children." *English Literary Renaissance*, 4 (1974), 315–325.

Raises questions and implications about staging a play for a boys' company. Marlowe's tragedy is "a carefully constructed vehicle" that displays the compatability of declamation and farce in drama and is thus dependent on child actors for its complete realization. The play is "a silly story superimposed upon the realities of passionate love and death," exploiting the potential of the boy actors. Such conditions, Cope suggests, could have also inspired *A Midsummer Night's Dream*.

297. Cutts, John P. "*Dido, Queen of Carthage*." *Notes and Queries*, NS 5 (1958), 371–374.

Claims that the virtues of the drama have been ignored and that it can "stand by itself" in interpretation. The opening love-scene between Jupiter and Ganymede is ironic because unlike mortals, time is under the gods' control. The scene contrasts with the ensuing mortal action and shows the "ironic mood of Marlowe's contempt" for "the authority of heaven which destroys the love affair of Dido and Aeneas."

298. ———. " 'By Shallow Rivers': A Study of Marlowe's *Dido, Queen of Carthage*. In *Studies in Medieval, Renaissance, and American Literature: A Festschrift Honoring Troy C. Crenshaw, Lorraine Sherley, and Ruth Speer*, pp. 73–94. Betsey F. Colquitt, ed. Fort Worth: Texas Christian University Press, 1971.

Aeneas is a weak figure whose gestures stem from "his feelings of inadequacy" both in the battlefield and in the bedroom. He is less than he should be, neither "epic, heroic, manly, [nor] vigorous." Dido's death in contrast is heroic and offsets our contempt for Aeneas' treason. (See also entry 95.)

299. Forbers, C. A. "Tragic Dido." *Classical Bulletin*, 29 (1953), 51–53; 58.

General account of Dido's appeal as a tragic figure.

299a. Geckle, George L. "The Wind of the Wound: Marlowe's *Dido, Queen of Carthage*, II.i.253–254." *Papers of the Bibliographical Society of America*, 71 (1977), 194–199.

Reconsiders the question of substituting "wound" for "wind" in Achilles' narration of the death of Priam. "Wound" was posited by Dyce in the last century; recent editions use the other reading.

300. Gibbons, Brian. "Unstable Proteus: Marlowe's *The Tragedy of Dido, Queen of Carthage*." In *Christopher Marlowe*, pp. 27–46. Brian Morris, ed. (See entry 170.)

Points out the play's emphasis on dramatic resources such

as costume, scenery, and spectacle, in addition to suggesting
hints in the language which show how Marlowe tailored the play
to a boys' company. While the play "may conclude in the exalta-
tion of the heroine . . . the play is not a unified heroic tragedy; we
must see it, rather, as a counterpoint of varying kinds of erotic
experience and attitudes to passion. It is this multiplicity which
we are called on to appreciate and which finally determines the
special quality of Marlowe's achievement" (p. 45).

300a. Gill, Roma. "Marlowe's Virgil: *Dido Queen of Carthage.*"
    Review of English Studies, 28 (1977), 141–155.
    Cogent analysis of Marlowe's adaptations from Virgil's
Aeneid for his play; which show his "detailed knowledge and easy
handling of his source" (141). Gill argues that the play's value
resides in revealing Marlowe's poetic talent; that unlike Shakespeare, whose basic unit for composing a play was a scene, Marlowe's plays emerge from units of poetry.

301. Godshalk, William L. "Marlowe's *Dido, Queen of Carth-
    age.*" *English Literary History,* 38 (1971), 1–18.
    Reasons for the neglect of the play are historical, i.e., the
identification of a dual authorship, which should be seen instead
by students of Marlowe and Nashe as "an excellent job of coor-
dinating their efforts." The opening scene suggests that "illegiti-
mate love is universal" and links the idea of fruitless love to Dido
and Aeneas. The gods do not control the action; rather, their behavior symbolizes the "inner realities" of human relationships.
From Jupiter to the Nurse, cutting across the universal scheme of
creation, Marlowe emphasizes the negative side of love which
forces the abandonment of social duties. There is no "tragic reso-
lution" in the play, "only the sense of recurrent destruction and
alienation."

302. Harrison, Thomas P., Jr. "Shakespeare and Marlowe's *Dido,
    Queen of Carthage. Studies in English* [University of Texas],
    36, (1956), 57–63.
    Points out analogies in *Antony and Cleopatra* to *Dido* in
pageantry, mood, and language.

303. Koskenniemi, Inna. "Did Marlowe Use Any Dramatic
    Sources for *Dido, Queen of Carthage?*" *Neuphilologische
    Mitteilungen,* 73 (1972), 143–152.

Suggests that Marlowe definitely knew Dolce's *Didone* (1547), and if not Cinthio's 1543 play about Dido, he at least knew for sure Cinthio's *Orbecche*, his best-known play, which contains a description of Priam's death.

304. Lambrichts, Guy. "Nashe et la *Didon* de Marlowe." *Bulletin de la Faculté des Lettres de Strasbourg*, 47 (1969), 181–188. [In French]

305. Lees, F. N. "*Dido, Queen of Carthage* and *The Tempest*." *Notes and Queries*, NS 11 (1964), 147–149.

Shakespeare may allude to the story in Marlowe's play in his "meditation on an ideal innocent enduring love-match" with patterns of "ill-fated love against which the ideal stands."

306. Maxwell, J. C. "Vergilian Half-Lines in Shakespeare's Heroic Narrative." *Notes and Queries*, 198 (1953), 100. Reference to Marlowe.

307. Pearce, T. M. "Evidence for Dating Marlowe's *Tragedy of Dido*." In *Studies in the English Renaissance Drama in Memory of Karl Julius Holzknecht*, pp. 231–247. New York University Press, 1959.

Argues that *Dido* was written after *Tamburlaine*, Parts I and II, on evidence of stage directions and the references to properties written into the lines of the play. The case for a later 1588–1591 date is strengthened by verbal similarities to Kyd's *The Spanish Tragedy* and to *Solimon and Perseda*.

308. Rogers, David M. "Love and Honor in Marlowe's *Dido, Queen of Carthage*." *Greyfriar*, 6 (1963), 3–7.

Fulfillment of love not compatible with pursuit of honor. In Marlowe's drama women are bound to the former, men to the latter. Those bound to love or to each other by passion are destroyed, while those who uphold honor succeed.

309. Rousseau, George S. "Marlowe's *Dido* and a Rhetoric of Love." *English Miscellany*, 19 (1968), 25–49.

Ethos, Logos, and Pathos are rhetorically employed by Marlowe to formally persuade the audience of the suffering of Dido and Aeneas. The rhetorical proficiency Marlowe displays in this early play helps to explain what made his "mighty line" mighty.

310. Smith, Mary Elizabeth. *"Love Kindling Fire": A Study of Christopher Marlowe's The Tragedy of Dido Queen of Carthage.* (Elizabethan and Renaissance Studies, 63) James Hogg, editor. Salzburg: Institut fur Englische Sprache und Literatur, 1977. 177 pp. + index.

The first book-length study of the play; Marlowe's problems of adaptation from classical and neo-classical sources; the requirements of boy actors; the relative artistic merits of *Dido* and its place in Marlowe's development.

311. ———. "Marlowe and Italian Dido Drama." *Italica*, 70 (1976), 223–235.

Documents six resemblances between Marlowe's play and Italian Renaissance dramatists; five "in the handling of plot and character and one unusual verbal parallel" (223). The Italian plays include Alessandro Pazzi's *Dido in Carthagine*, 1524; Cinthio's *Didone*, 1543; and Docle's *Didone*, 1547. This article strengthens the case that Marlowe was familiar with Italian dramatic versions of the story.

312. ———. "Staging Marlowe's *Dido Queene of Carthage*." *Studies in English Literature*, 17 (1977), 177–190.

A fascinating and plausible recreation of a "performance" of *Dido* that reveals Marlowe's attempt "to cope with changing fashions and tastes which were beginning to veer away from the highly specialized techniques used in the private theaters. . . . If *Dido* is at fault for straying sometimes outside the accepted limitations of child-theater, it suffers from the very same qualities which become strengths in the plays for the public theater." Smith thinks that even in its own time, despite its virtues, *Dido* would not have secured a fully successful play to Marlowe's first audiences.

313. Tinker, Michael. "*Dido, Queen of Carthage* and the Children's Companies of the 1580's." *DAI*, 36 (1976), 2859A. (University of Wisconsin-Madison)

314. Xavier, Francis. "Christopher Marlowe's *Dido, Queen of Carthage*." *DAI*, 33 (1972), 1702A. (University of Ohio)

315. Young, Steven C. *The Frame Structure in Tudor and Stuart Drama.* (Salzburg Studies in English Literature under the Direction of Professor Erwin A. Stürzl, No. 6) Salzburg: Institut für Englishce Sprache und Literatur, Universität Salzburg. 1974. v + 189 pp. See esp. Chapter IV, "Marlowe, *Dido, Queen of Carthage*," pp. 47–62.

Identifies as a structural device a "dramatic frame," a "complete dramatic action within which the presentation of a full-length play occurs as an event." Containing at least two spoken parts, it occurs "on a different narrative plane" than the major play action, as in *Dido*, where the frame encompasses the supernatural exchanges of the gods. Thus the "broken promise" operates both on Olympus and at Carthage, and the principals in the human tragedy reflect conflicts between Zeus and Juno.

5. EDWARD II

316. Ahrends, Günter. "Die Bildersprache in Marlowe's *Edward II.*" *Germanisch-romanisch Monatschafte,* Neue Folge 19 (1969), 353–379. [In German]
    A lengthy analysis of imagery in a play where it is generally thought to be subdued and muted.

317. Bowers, Fredson. "Was There a Lost 1593 Edition of Marlowe's *Edward II?*" *Studies in Bibliography,* 25 (1972), 143–148.
    There answer is *no.* 1594 represents the earliest edition of the play. See also p. 4 of Bowers' edition of Marlowe's *Complete Works* (entry 8).

318. Brodwin, Leonora Leet. "*Edward II:* Marlowe's Culminating Treatment of Love." *English Literary History,* 31 (1964), 139–155.
    Marlowe does not find love an "inspiring" subject so long as it involves women as its object; usually his heroes find love "degrading and even damning [*Dr. Faustus*]" but in *Edward II,* Marlowe was able to present it in terms of homosexual love and thus to realize his empathy and vision. In *Edward II,* this love is a "saving value." Edward is able to accept the loss of his crown "because it has been the price of a dedication to love which he still affirms as the highest value of his existence."

319. Ceccio, Joseph F. "Marlowe's *Edward II:* A Revaluation." *DAI,* 36 (1975), 2840A. (University of Illinois, Urbana-Champaign)

320. Fricker, Robert H. "The Dramatic Structure of *Edward II.*" *English Studies,* 34 (1953), 203–217. Reprinted in Ribner (entry 26), pp. 128–144.
    This play differs from Marlowe's other plays in not being loose and episodic; nor does a single character in it dominate all

the action; nor is it characterized by spectacular verse. *Edward II* is rather constructed with its emphasis on conflict and interplay between characters; its structure is dynamic, like Shakespeare's *2 and 3 Henry VI* plays. The resulting drama is tightly woven, its principal tragic rhythms intensify as the conflicts move toward conclusion.

321. Godshalk, William L. "Marlowe and Lucan." *Notes and Queries*, NS 18 (1971), 13.

The author notes three echoes in *Edward II* from Lucan's Civil Wars, Book II; these are I.i, 173; I.iv, 102–103; and IV.v, 60.

322. Hattaway, Michael. "Marlowe and Brecht." In *Christopher Marlowe*, pp. 95–112. Brian Morris, ed. (See entry 170.)

"Marlowe's plays work in large part by irony, by alienation as much as by identification. . . . Marlowe is one of the most intellectual of the Elizabethans in that he offers his audience a number of clearly defined choices" (p. 97). Hattaway's discussion does not necessarily center on *Edward II*, but embraces other major plays as well. Like Marlowe, Brecht is fairly didactic and both dramatists present images in a living way; that is, characters embody ideas, actors are not seen as fellow human beings. Both elicit complex and controlled responses from their audiences.

323. Hill, James J. "Critical Studies of Christopher Marlowe's *Edward II*." *DAI*, 27 (1966), 4221A. (University of Texas at Austin)

324. Hirsch, Richard S. M. "A Second Echo of *Edward II* in *1 Henry.IV*." *Notes and Queries*, NS 22 (1975), 168.

I.iiii, 233—an image of a poisoned drink in Shakespeare's play—derived from II.ii, 237–238 in Marlowe's.

325. Johnson, S. F. "Marlowe's *Edward II*." *Explicator*, 10 (1952), item 53.

Discusses musical images and allusions.

326. Kurokawa, Takashi. "De Casibus Tragedy and Machiavellism—in Connection with the Theme of *Edward II*." *Shakespeare Studies*, 7 [Japan] (1968–1969), 61–80.

Examines the central conflict between Edward on the one

hand and Mortimer, the Queen, and their allies on the other, as
representative of a clash of ideals: Edward's personal devotion is
rendered in terms of *de casibus* tragedy; his opponents are ma-
nipulative politicians interested only in power.

327. Labouille, Louise J. "A Note on Bertold Brecht's Adaptation
of Marlowe's *Edward II.*" *Modern Language Review*, 54
(1959), 214–220.
    Brecht tailors historical fact to polemical ends and thus
sacrifices the eloquence and pathos in Marlowe's original. What
saves the Brecht version is its depiction of human wretchedness,
inspired and extended from Marlowe's play.

328. Leech, Clifford. "Marlowe's *Edward II:* Power and Suffering." *Critical Quarterly*, 1 (1959), 181–196. Originally the
Ann Elizabeth Sheble Lecture, Bryn Mawr College, 17
November 1958. (Reprinted in entries 22, 26 and 177.)
    The play's emphasis is on the suffering men cause in their
lust for power; Marlowe has no real moral purpose except to depict "ultimate suffering" in order to bring home a basic truth
about part of human nature.

329. Perret, Marion. "Edward III: Marlowe's Dramatic Technique." *Review of English Literature*, 7:4 (1966), 87–91.
    The Prince of Wales in *Edward II*, who becomes king
when his father is deposed, is the mirror and standard by which
the shortcomings of adults are seen.

330. Ribner, Irving. "Marlowe's *Edward II* and the Tudor History Play." *English Literary History*, 22 (1955), 243–253.
(See also his discussion in entry 195, 123–133.)
    Argues that *Edward II* is a mature tragedy of character
that is based on Marlowe's essentially classical view of history.
This view of history, with its emphasis on individual accomplishment and will, is darkened here as compared to the early plays
because, Ribner says, it is accompanied by the disintegration of
the king's character. The play exhibits political themes that seem
important to Marlowe: the relationship between king and nobility
demands that the absolute ruler govern justly; Edward does not;
virtù alone, as the fall of Mortimer indicates, is not sufficient to
assure political success; the relationship of nobility to birth is
slight.

331. Robertson, Toby. "Directing *Edward II.*" *Tulane Drama Review*, 8:4 (1964), 174–183.
An interview with John Russell Brown on a modern production of the play.

332. Summers, Claude J. "Isabella's Plea for Gaveston in Marlowe's *Edward II.*" *Philological Quarterly*, 52 (1973), 308–310.
Isabella's plea is neither simple nor abject; she is not the innocent suffering queen she makes herself out to be. Her plea provides the subtle pretext on which the nobles carry out their murder of Gaveston. She is, therefore, not inconsistently drawn by Marlowe, but a scheming Machiavel.

333. Sunesen, Bent. "Marlowe and the Dumb Show." *English Studies*, 35 (1954), 241–253.
Gaveston's opening soliloquy is a verbal enactment of a dumb show that prefigures the ensuing action; and in reiterating its substance in *Edward II*, Marlowe makes it "the nucleus of his dramatic structure."

334. Wada, Yuichi. "Edward II as Tragic Hero." *Studies in English Literature*, 41 (1964), 1–17. [Japan; in English]
Argues for the essential dignity of Marlowe's protagonist, showing how he lends this unpopular, effeminate king a measure of stature that stirs audience sympathies.

335. Waith, Eugene M. "*Edward II:* The Shadow of Action." *Tulane Drama Review*, 8:4 (1964), 59–76. Reprinted in Ribner (entry 26), pp. 175–191.
The structure of the play may be graphically described as the intersection of five lines, "each corresponding to the rising and falling fortunes of a major character." As the play progresses, Marlowe concentrates the emotional energy of the drama so that its "utmost confinement produces the maximal emotional response" (65). The play's emphasis is on pathos and horror.

336. Weisstein, Ulrich. "The First Version of Brecht/ Feuchtwanger's *Leben Edwards des Zweiten von England* and Its Relation to the Standard Text." *Journal of English and Germanic Philology*, 69 (1970), 193–210.

Deals incidentally with Marlowe's play as the author explores the early version of Brecht's work.

337. ————. "Marlowe's Homecoming, or *Edward II* crosses the Atlantic." *Monatschafte*, 60 (1968), 234–242.
A lengthy and highly critical review of Eric Bentley's American-English translation of Brecht's adaptation of Marlowe.

338. Welsh, Robert Ford. "The Printer of the 1594 Octavo of Marlowe's *Edward II*." *Studies in Bibliography*, 17 (1964), 197–198.
Richard Bradock, who printed the 1598 edition of the play, cannot be responsible for the 1594 text. Ornaments used by Bradock in 1598 belonged to Robert Robinson in 1594, whose widow Bradock soon married.

339. Wickham, Glynne. "Shakespeare's *Richard II* and Marlowe's *Edward II*." In *Shakespeare's Dramatic Heritage* (See entry 234), pp. 165–179. Also reprinted in Ribner (entry 26), pp. 199–212.
Believes that Marlowe's conception of tragic events in *Edward II* is Aristotelean; the king a hero whose hamartia is "his inability to observe that discretion in his relations with Gaveston urged on him by his peers."

6. DOCTOR FAUSTUS

340. Alexander, Nigel. *The Performance of Christopher Marlowe's Doctor Faustus*. London: Oxford University Press, 1971. 19 pp. See also *Procedings of the British Academy, 57* (1974), 331–349.

Defends the integrity of the whole play [B-text] and sees it working as a "suspense film" where Mephistopheles provides the spectators with the information necessary to arouse tension regarding the play's outcome. Reviewed by Roma Gill, *Notes and Queries*, NS 21 (1974), 309.

341. Baker, Donald C. "Ovid and Faustus: The *Noctis Equi*." *Classical Journal*, 55 (1959), 126–128.

Marlowe's adaptation of Ovid's line from the *Amores* (I, 13, 1.40) in Faustus' final speech is the most interesting line in the tragedy. Faustus' whole life has been a night of the soul and he is, ironically, the "hardened sensualist" who goes to his doom.

342. Barber, C. L. "The Form of Faustus' Fortunes Good or Bad." *Tulane Drama Review*, 8:4 (1964), 92–119. Reprinted in entry 33, pp. 173–199.

Marlowe, writes Barber in his influential article, dramatizes blasphemy, but "not with the single perspective of a religious point of view: he dramatizes blasphemy as heroic endeavor. The play is an expression of the Reformation;... Marlowe makes blasphemy a Promethean enterprise, heroic and tragic, an expression of the Renaissance" (92). The conflict in the play is utterly dramatic; the gulf between tragic desire and frequently debunked comic attainment is held together by magnificent poetry.

343. Baumgart, Wolfgang. "Prospero." In *Festschrift für Richard Alewyn*, pp. 84–102. Herbert Singer, Benno von Weise, eds. Cologne: Böhlau, 1967.

Some reference to Marlowe's hero in contrast.

344. Beall, Charles N. "Definition of Theme by Unconsecutive Event: Structure as Induction in Marlowe's *Doctor Faustus*." *Renaissance Papers*, (1962), 53–61.

The time elapsed from Faustus' fall in the beginning of the play through his death and damnation at its end may be seen as an experiment in induction conducted by Marlowe with his audience. Events not only exhibit the play's theme, but actually fulfill it.

345. Bensen, Robert R. "The Under-achiever: a Study of Marlowe's *Doctor Faustus*." *Studies in The Humanities* 3:1 (1972), 40–42.

Marlowe's hero is no Renaissance man but a dupe.

346. Blackburn, William. "'Heavenly Words': Marlowe's Faustus as a Renaissance Magician." *English Studies in Canada*, 4:1 (1978), 1–14.

Provides an analysis of Faustus' "one attempt at magic before he signs the pact with Lucifer" and its context in Renaissance magic. Marlowe's concept of magic is drawn upon the Protean magic found in works such Pico's *Oration* (1486), which Marlowe assimilates in the play to show that Faustus is ignorant of magic. This ignorance is the play's central metaphor and is seen in the hero's lack of truly understanding language. Faustus is a poor scholar whose career, we realize, presents "the species of a man of great promise and noble aspiration who has destroyed himself through failure to master the power that language provides."

347. Bluestone, Max. "*Libido Speculandi:* Doctrine and Dramaturgy in Contemporary Interpretations of *Doctor Faustus*." In *Reinterpretations of Elizabethan Drama. Selected Papers of the English Institute, 1968,* pp. 33–88. Norman Rabkin, ed. New York: Columbia University Press, 1969.

Surely one of the best essays of its kind; a perceptive and sensitive analysis of the trends in criticism of the play. Bluestone's major claim and his major objection to the course of much recent interpretation is that in their pursuit of doctrine—orthodox Christianity and Renaissance skepticism and heterodoxy—and in their identification of Marlowe with the central character of his play, critics have overlooked the theatricality and effectiveness of *Doctor Faustus* on the stage.

348. Bowe, Elaine C. "Doctrines and Images of Despair in Christopher Marlowe's *Doctor Faustus* and Edmund Spenser's *The Faerie Queene*." *DAI*, 29 (1969), 2206A. (University of Oregon)

349. Bowers, Fredson. "Marlowe's *Dr. Faustus:* The 1602 Additions." *Studies in Bibliography*, 26 (1973), 1–18.
  Questions Greg's assumption that additions were work of early revision (presumably by Marlowe) that are present in the B-text. Bowers claims that the 1602 additions present in the B-text were by Rowley and Birde; Marlowe's play is best represented by the A-text. (See entry 8, pp. 128–129 [Volume II].)

350. ———. "The Text of Marlowe's *Faustus*." *Modern Philology*, 49 (1952), 195–204.
  A review of Greg's great parallel text edition (entry 30); presents a case for its various weaknesses and oversights. Bowers concludes, however, that with Greg's edition, "the play in its major features is a problem no longer."

351. Bowers, R. H. "Marlowe's *Dr. Faustus*, Tirso's *El condenado por desconfiado*, and the Secret Cause." *Costerus*, 4 (1972), 9–27.

352. Bradbrook, Muriel C. "Marlowe's *Doctor Faustus* and the Eldritch Tradition." In *Essays on Shakespeare and Elizabethan Drama in Honor of Hardin Craig*, pp. 83–90. Richard Hosley, ed. Columbia, Missouri: University of Missouri Press, 1962.
  Bradbrook means by "eldritch tradition" the diabolism of cackling witches and goblins which is "comic and horrific, is amoral and does not involve personal choice or the notion of personal responsibility" (p. 83). She traces the tradition back to medieval drama and mummings to help make the middle of Marlowe's drama "more explicable, if not more acceptable." She contends that the comic ghoulishness of the folk heightens our awareness of "the fine and sensitive mind lured to self-destruction with the gross simplicity that has not yet reached the level of making a moral choice" (p. 90).

353. Brockbank, Philip. *Marlowe: Doctor Faustus.* (Studies in English Literature, No. 6) David Daiches, General Editor.

London: Edward Arnold, and Great Neck, N.Y.: Barron's Educational Series, 1962. 62 pp.

An in-depth analysis of the entire play with some critical apparatus, designed for the advanced and general students of the play alike. "Perspectives of Criticism" provides a topical survey of major issues informing the background of *Doctor Faustus,* ranging from "From Simon Magus to Faustus" to "Marlowe and Renaissance Italy" (pp. 9–29), and a thorough explication of the drama (pp. 30–60). An appendix on text and sources is also included. Brockbank writes towards the end (p. 59) that "Faustus' ordeal is specifically that of an aspiring mind. . . of that part of our own nature which is dissatisfied with being merely human and tries vainly to come to rest in fantasies of omnipotence and omniscience. It is a romantic agony which oscillates . . . between extremities of hope and despair. Marlowe . . . related the hope to the imperial and speculative ambitions of his time, and the despair to that side of Christianity which brings home to us the inescapable mortality and doom of man."

354. Brooke, Nicholas. "The Moral Tragedy of Doctor Faustus." *Cambridge Journal,* 7 (1952), 662–687. (Reprinted in entry 177.)

Brooke sees the play as an inverted morality. Faustus is a Tamburlanian hero whose right to challenge human limitations is poised in direct conflict with submission to powers greater than the individual. Attacks the Greg and Kirschbaum reconstructions of the play, which he insists downplay the morality trappings and reduce the "tragic certainty of the conclusion." Like others, Brooke notes that the greatest speeches in the play are those spoken against accepted Christian morality.

355. Brown, P. W. F. "Saint Clement and Doctor Foster." *Notes and Queries,* NS 1 (1954), 140–141.

The original Faust or Foster—a necromancer—was the supposed father of St. Clement.

356. Burwick, Frederick. "Marlowe's *Doctor Faustus:* Two Manners, the Argumentative and the Passionate." *Neuphilologische Mitteilungen,* 70 (1969), 121–145.

The conflict between logos and pathos in the character of the hero makes Faustus sympathetic and provides the key to the tragic tension experienced by auditors and readers.

357. Cameron, Kenneth W. "Transcendental Hell in Emerson and Marlowe." *Emerson Society Quarterly*, 6 (1957), 9–10. Reference to *Doctor Faustus*.

358. Campbell, Lily Bess. "*Doctor Faustus*: A Case of Conscience." *Publications of the Modern Language Association*, 67 (1952), 219–239.
Suggests that the Marlowe play may in part be based on the case of Francesco Spiera, a sixteenth-century figure who was believed damned for despair. Campbell argues that the hero in the play is not damned at the outset and that the morality elements of the play are really Reformation concerns that unify the tragedy.

359. Carpenter, Nan C. "'Miles' versus 'Clericus' in Marlowe's *Faustus*." *Notes and Queries*, 197 (1952), 91–93.
Faustus' discomfiture of the skeptical knight seen as "dramatizing the prestige of the scholar at the social and intellectual level," thus binding comic actions to the main plot. Marlowe follows tradition by allowing the scholar to best the soldier (Faustus over Benvolio).

360. ———. "Music in *Doctor Faustus*. Two Notes." *Notes and Queries*, 195 (1950), 180–181.
1. The singing of the dirge by the Friars reminds audience of "coming death and eternal damnation" for Faustus, even as the text of the dirge, a catalogue of curses, satirizes "the lavishness of ecclesiastical living." 2. Faustus' lines 637–641 derive from the *English Faustbook*.

361. Carroll, Jane Z. "A Defense of Marlowe's Faustus." *English Record*, 12:2 (1961), 39–42.
Compares Faustus to Macbeth in order to show that Marlowe's hero, though sharing Macbeth's ambition and wilfulness, is more restrained in his use of power and possesses greater intellect.

362. Cole, Douglas, "Faust and Anti-Faust in Modern Drama." *Drama Survey*, 5 (1966), 39–52.
Comparative survey with some incidental reference to Marlowe.

363. Cooper, Barbara. "An Ur-*Faustus?*" *Notes and Queries*, NS 6 (1959), 66–68.

References in Prynne's *Histio Mastix* (1633) and Stubbs *Anatomy of Abuse* (1595) both refer to an earthquake that occurred during a performance of a play; Middleton's *The Blacke Book* (1604) refers to such an event occurring during *Doctor Faustus:* the quake in question occurred on 6 April, 1580. Conjectural evidence for an earlier version of Marlowe's play by another writer.

364. Cox, Gerald H., III. "Marlowe's Doctor Faustus and 'Sin against the Holy Ghost'." *Huntington Library Quarterly*, 36 (1973), 119–137.

The play follows the three-art division of the chapbook—devil, world, and flesh. Underlying the temptations are sins of presumption, despair, unrepentance, obstinacy, resistance to known truth, envy of others' spiritual good—all sins against the Holy Ghost. Cox feels the underpinning Marlowe thus employs makes the play unambiguous and, in Christian terms, tragic.

365. Crabtree, John H., Jr. "The Comedy in Marlowe's *Doctor Faustus.*" *Furman Studies*, 9:1 (1961), 1–9.

Claims that the comic scenes are integral regardless of ultimate attribution and in accord with contemporary theatrical practices.

366. Craik, T. W. "Fraustus' Damnation Reconsidered." *Renaissance Drama*, NS 2 (1969), 189–196.

Reply to Greg's 1946 essay: Craik says that "repent" and "spirit" are used in the play in both precise (Christian) and loose colloquial senses.

367. Crundell, H. W. "Nashe and *Doctor Faustus.*" *Notes and Queries*, NS 9 (1962), 327.

Provides an additional bit of verbal evidence to strengthen the case that the comic scenes in Marlowe's play (III.iii.) bear a likeness to Nashe's *Lenten Stuffe,* and were penned in *Faustus* by Marlowe's old collaborator from Cambridge days.

368. Davidson, Clifford. "Doctor Faustus at Rome." *Studies in English Literature*, 9 (169), 231–239.

Roman episodes in the B-text seem to favor Marlowe's authorship because the popish satire in the play recalls the action in *The Jew of Malta* especially, and because Faustus in one sense can be seen as the force of Protestant good challenging the authority and pomposity of the Pope.

369. ———. "Doctor Faustus of Wittenberg." *Studies in Philology*, 59 (1962), 514–523.
   Claims that theology of Wittenberg Reformers as recorded by Melancthon in his *Loci Commenes* (1521) informs the ideas of the play. The reformers believed that a man's deeds for better or worse were insufficient to achieve salvation—God must intervene. Marlowe's hero suffers from a misdirected will that prevents his acceptance of grace.

370. Deats, Sara M. "*Doctor Faustus:* From Chapbook to Tragedy." *Essays in Literature*, 3:1 (1976), 3–16.
   Examines afresh (see entry 371) the relationship between the play and *The English Faustbook* (1592) in order to show Marlowe's crucial alterations and translations to suit the dramatic medium, including those which accentuate "the vast disparity between the omnipotence of Faustus' dream and the impotence of his reward"; those which affirm "concepts of volition and responsibility which form the moral fulcrum of both play and source"; where the emphasis in the play is less on the physical than on the psychological "dilaceration of the human personality by sin."

371. ———. "Marlowe's *Doctor Faustus:* From Chapbook to Tragedy." *DAI*, 32 (1971), 385A. (University of California, Los Angeles)

372. Dent, R. W. "Ramist Faustus or Ramist Marlowe?" In *Studies Presented to Tanno F. Mustanoja on the Occasion of His Sixtieth Birthday. Neuphilologische Mitteilungen*, 73 (1972), 63–74.
   Explicates academic jokes in the opening soliloquy.

373. Deyermond, A. D. "Skelton and the Epilogue to Marlowe's *Doctor Faustus.*" *Notes and Queries*, NS 10 (1963), 410–411.
   The opening lines of the play's epilogue resemble John

Skelton's *The Garlands of Laurell* (15–21), showing Marlowe's awareness of earlier Tudor poets.

374. Duthie, G. I. "Some Observations on Marlowe's *Doctor Faustus.*" *Archiv für das Studium der neuren Sprachen und Literaturen*, 203 (1966), 81–96.
      Sees the play as orthodox and asserting traditional Christian morality; the play's most florid speeches—seen by some as evidence of Marlowe's sympathies with his rebellious hero—are not at odds with the Christian outlook of the drama, especially the Helen speech.

375. Elton, William. "'Shore's Wife and *Doctor Faustus.*" *Notes and Queries*, 195 (1950), 526. (See entry 415.)
      Allusion to Marlowe's play anticipated in *MLN*, 38 (1923), 82–92.

376. Fabian, Bernard. "Marlowe's *Doctor Faustus.*" *Notes and Queries*, NS 3 (1956), 56–57.
      Play's second line means: Where fortune in war [Mars] joined [did mate] the Carthaginians.

377. ———. "A Note on Marlowe's *Faustus.*" *English Studies*, 41 (1960), 365–368.
      Confounding hell in Elysium is Virgilian not Averroist (cf. *Aeneid*, VI, 540–543). [See entries 445–446.]

378. Farnham, Willard ed. *Twentieth Century Interpretations of Doctor Faustus.* Englewood Cliffs, N.J.: Prentice Hall, 1969. vi + 120 pp.
      Reprints essays or excerpts from studies by 20 authors, including older essays by George Santayana (1910), M. C. Bradbrook (1935, see entry 72), James Smith (1939), and Helen Gardner (1948) as well as Frye and Sewell (see 382 and 440 below) and Levin (156), Cole (90), Kirschbaum (10), Steane (218), and Knights (142).

378a. Fitz, L. T. "'More than Thou Hast Wit to Ask': Marlowe's Faustus as Numskull." *Folklore*, 88 (1977), 215–219.
      Although the real Faustus had a reputation as a swindler, Marlowe's hero is a dupe, swindled in his deed of gift for his soul

as seen in II.ii.69–75. Furthermore, the action of the play may be seen in the context of the traditional tale of the wasted wish or foolish bargain. These stories often emphasize the shallow materialism of the main character. Marlowe's hero is not the epitome of an aspiring mind; he is rather "a sixteenth-century numskull" (219).

379. French, A. L. "The Philosophy of *Dr. Faustus.*" *Essays in Criticism*, 20 (1970), 123–142.

Maintains that the hero is presented ironically, but that this presentation destroys the play. The man billed in the Prologue as a great academician undoes himself in the first scene; he is neither a scholar nor an intellectual. Marlowe cannot present the causes of his hero's damnation; Faustus imagines himself damned before even signing the bond. The long-held respect for Marlowe's play since the last century ought to be dispelled by its flagrant inconsistencies.

380. French, William W. "The Double View in *Doctor Faustus.*" *West Virginia University Philogoical Papers*, 17 (1970), 3–15.

The play's serio-comic rhythm provides a double view of the main themes. These are alternation between optimism and pessimism about man's abilities and the justice or injustice of divine power from man's perspective.

381. Frey, Leonard H. "Antithetical Balance in the Opening and Close of *Doctor Faustus.*" *Modern Language Quarterly*, 24 (1963), 350–353.

The two soliloquies exhibit one theme—self-confidence, only in the second speech this demeanor is supplanted by submissiveness before the forces of the cosmos.

382. Frye, Roland Mushat. "Marlowe's *Doctor Faustus:* The Repudiation of Humanity." *South Atlantic Quarterly*, 55 (1956), 322–328.

Faustus' sin is usurping divinity while simultaneously rejecting humanity in a Calvinist sense. This theme informs all of the actions of the play. (Reprinted in 378.)

383. Gilbert, Allan H. "'A Thousand Ships'." *Modern Language Notes*, 67 (1951), 477–478.

Possible source not only Lucian (*Dialogues of the Dead*, 18) but also *The Agamemnon* of Seneca (171–173) and incidentally in the *Troades*.

384. Goldfarb, Russell and Clare. "The Seven Deadly Sins in *Doctor Faustus*." *College Language Association Journal*, 13 (1970), 350–363.
    This essay argues that the sins are an ironic diversion for Faustus in the context of the play's action because he is truly ignorant of sin.

385. Goldman, Arnold. "'The Fruitful Plot of Scholarism Graced'." *Notes and Queries*, NS 11 (1964), 264.
    The phrase refers to *divinity*, not Faustus, and takes its significance by highlighting the difference between pursuits of knowledge sacred and profane.

386. Gonzalez, LaVerne D. K. "The Faustian Motif in Genet: A Comparison of Marlowe's *Doctor Faustus* and Genet's *Notre-Dame-des-Fleurs*." *DAI*, 33 (1972), 723A. (Purdue University)

387. Grigson, Georffrey. "'The Topless Towers'." *TLS*, 23 April, 1964, p. 343.
    Did Marlowe know the *Troy Book*, published in French editions in 1490, 1510, & 1544, which refers to "the toplesse Towres of Illium" under a full-page woodcut of The Trojan Horse?

388. Grotowski, Jerzy. "*Doctor Faustus* in Poland." *Tulane Drama Review*, 8:4 (1964), 120–133.
    Reviews trends in recent productions and popularity of Marlowe's play.

389. Haile, H. G. *The History of Dr. Johann Faustus: Recorded from the German*. Urbana: University of Illinois Press, 1965. 135 pp.
    A scholarly edition of the Faust chapbook.

390. Hart, Jeffrey P. "Prospero and Faustus." *Boston University Studies in English*, 2 (1956), 197–206.

An interesting essay in contrast between Shakespeare and Marlowe and Greene, pointing out that Prospero's magic tends towards muscial harmony where Faustus' tends towards fire; unlike Prospero, Faustus loses himself and his soul because he cannot renounce his art.

391. Hattaway, Michael. "The Theology of Marlowe's *Doctor Faustus.*" *Renaissance Drama*, NS 3 (1970), 51–78.
   Play is an ironical reversal of the story of Solomon, the Biblical exemplar of wisdom, whose intellectual content is based largely on Renaissance skepticism and Protestant fideism. Comic scenes are integral to show that Faustus is obtuse, incapable of acknowledging mysteries beyond the material and sensual existence.

392. Hawkins, Sherman. "The Education of Faustus." *Studies in English Literature*, 6 (1966), 193–209.
   At first, Faust knows about sin in abstract or objective senses through books; he eventually experiences sin firsthand until his knowledge of evil is so pronounced that he cuts himself off from redemption.

393. Heller, Erich. "Faust's Damnation: The Morality of Knowledge." *Listener*, 11 January, 1962, pp. 60–62. (Reprinted in entry 28).
   Marlowe's hero, like the sciences and humanistic studies, asserts life. The play and the legend warn us against using our knowledge to make a hell of our own.

394. Homan, Sidney R. "*Doctor Faustus,* Dekker's *Old Fortunatus*, and the Mortality Plays." *Modern Language Quarterly*, 26 (1965), 497–505.
   Dekker's play relies heavily on Marlowe's but its morality play elements, unlike those in *Faustus*, are not subordinate to the central theme, which is the destruction of an extraordinary man.

395. Honderich, Pauline, "John Calvin and Doctor Faustus." *Modern Language Review*, 68 (1973), 1–13.
   Marlowe's knowledge of Calvinism creates psychological realism of the protagonist's character who vacillates between re-

pentance and defiance. Honderich makes a strong case for Marlowe's knowledge of basic Calvinist literature.

396. Hoy, Cyrus. "'Ignorance in Knowledge': Marlowe's Faustus and Ford's Giovanni." *Modern Philology,* 57 (1960), 145–154.

Ford's play *'Tis Pity She's a Whore* is indebted to Marlowe's because both heroes dabble in taboos, both misuse their powers of reason in pursuit of their respective passions whose damning consequences they face with impunity.

397. Hunter, G. K. "The Five-Act Structure in *Doctor Faustus.*" *Tulane Drama Review,* 8:4 (1964), 77–91.

The play as we have it is carefully planned. The hierarchical structure of human enquiry and knowledge forms the frame for Faustus' moral and spiritual decline, as seen by his participation in the subplot as well as in the main Wittenberg plot.

398. Jackson, M. P. "Three Old Ballads and the Date of *Doctor Faustus.*" *AUMLA,* 36 (1971), 187–200.

Dates Marlowe's play from 1588/89.

399. Jantz, Harold. "An Elizabethan Statement on the Origin of the German Faust Book, with a Note on Marlowe's Sources." *Journal of English and Germanic Philology,* 51 (1952), 137–153.

Argues that the first book referred to in the *Second Report of Dr. John Faustus* (1594) was the German folk book published in 1587. The later version was translated from a Latin original perhaps known to Marlowe in that form.

400. Jensen, Enjer J. "Heroic Convention and *Doctor Faustus.*" *Essays in Criticism,* 21 (1971), 101–106.

A reply to French (379) which claims that the ambiguities and contradictions in Marlowe's hero are keys to the greatness of the work as a dramatic tragedy.

401. Jump, John D. "Spenser and Marlowe." *Notes and Queries,* NS 11 (1964), 261–262.

The Faerie Queene, III, x, 46 and Marlowe's play B_1B_1 v. in 1604 text.

402. ———, ed. *Marlowe: Doctor Faustus: A Casebook.* London: Macmillan, 1969.

Reprints a selection from books and articles of criticism of the play.

403. Kahler, Erich. "Doctor Faustus from Adam to Sartre." *Comparative Drama,* 1 (1967), 75–92.

Sees Marlowe's play as the first attempt to present the conflict between conventional Christian wisdom and the "rational enlightenment gradually uprooting it."

404. Kaula, David. "Time and Timelessness in *Everyman* and *Doctor Faustus.*" *College English,* 22 (1960), 9–14.

Everyman is Catholic in perspective; Faustus is Protestant. In the former, the hero, who represents all of humanity, is saved; while in the latter Faustus the individual is damned. Marlowe's play is acutely aware of the differences between our sense of temporal and eternal time schemes.

405. Kesler, Charlotte. "The Importance of the Comic Tradition in English Drama in the Interpretation of Marlowe's *Doctor Faustus.*" *DAI,* 15 (1955), 1387–1388. (University of Missouri)

406. Kiessling, Nicolas. "Doctor Faustus and the Sin of Demonality." *Studies in English Literature,* 15 (1975), 205–211.

Argues against Greg's 1946 essay—which claims that Faustus is damned for his sexual intercourse with Helen, who is a succubus—because medieval records support the idea that any sin, no matter how heinous, was pardonable. Thus, Faustus does not lose his soul once and for all with Helen.

407. Kuriyama, Constance Brown. "Dr. Greg and *Doctor Faustus:* The Supposed Originality of the 1616 Text." *English Literary Renaissance,* 5 (1975), 171–197.

Despite flaws in the *A-text* it is "aesthetically superior" to *B* and fresh stylistic analysis confirms at least Rowley's partial authorship of comic scenes. The fully original form of the play has been lost and, while the *A-text* may be better from the standpoint of general readers and critics, the B-additions remain.

408. Lancashire, Anne. "*Timon of Athens:* Shakespeare's *Doctor Faustus.*" *Shakespeare Quarterly,* 21 (1970), 35–44.

Timon is like *Faustus* as a "secularized anti-traditional morality play" and presents the destruction of the protagonist in a pattern of action that is founded on morality play traditions.

409. Langston, Beach. "Marlowe's *Faustus* and the *Ars Moriendi* Tradition." In Arnold Williams, ed. *A Tribute to George Coffin Taylor: Studies and Essays, Chiefly Elizabethan, by His Students and Friends,* pp. 148–167. Chapel Hill: University of North Carolina Press, 1952.

Marlowe's play accepts the psychological and theological elements of the *ars moriendi* tradition, but rejects all trappings of its rituals. Of the contempt of the world element of the tradition, "Marlowe not only accepted nothing whatever; he even affirmed all that it denied." What he employs in the play from the tradition becomes a way of depicting the torments in Faustus' soul.

410. Longo, Joseph A. "Marlowe's *Doctor Faustus:* Allegorical Parody in Act Five." *Greyfriar,* 15 (1974), 38–49.

Parodies and inversions of the Passion turn Faustus into an anti-Christ who is torn between Hope and Despair.

411. Lynner, Darwin T., II. "The Dramatic Form of Christopher Marlowe's *Doctor Faustus.*" *DAI,* 33 (1973), 4352A. (S.U.N.Y. at Buffalo)

412. McAlindon, T. "Classical Mythology and Christian Tradition in Marlowe's *Doctor Faustus.*" *Publications of the Modern Language Association,* 81 (1966), 214–223.

Allusions to myths in the play not decorative; rather, they suggest Faustus' essential paganism that opens the way for his abjuration of theology in favor of magic.

413. McCullen, Joseph T. "Dr. Faustus and Renaissance Learning." *Modern Language Review,* 51 (1956), 6–16.

Faustus' want of knowledge is the cause of his rebellion and later of his despair. His intellectual blindness has led him to ignorance of himself. For too long he is unaware of his ignorance.

414. Manley, Frank. "The Nature of Faustus." *Modern Philology,* 66 (1969), 218–231.

Play leaves its central paradox unresolved. Faustus is mortal—but a man—and yet has an immortal spirit. He is free to act and yet renders himself incapable of acting for repentance. His central problem is that of identity; like other tragic heroes, this search for identity causes his tragic isolation.

415. Martin, Betty C. "*Shore's Wife* as a Source of the Epilogue of *Doctor Faustus.*" *Notes and Queries*, 195 (1950), 182.
Churchyard's contribution of the life of Jane Shore to *The Mirror for Magistrates* contains in 11, 139–140 a parallel to Marlowe's epilogue. (See entry 375.)

416. Matalene, H. W., III. "Marlowe's *Faustus* and the Comforts of Academicism." *English Literary History*, 39 (1972), 495–519.
Sees the protagonist as shallow, his sense of worth as dependent upon "being superficial." His books are props to make him "feel smart" and he tries to realize his self-worth by immersion in magic. He lacks the will, however, not to be dominated by his pursuits. His jokes are thus natural developments of the play, not glaringly out of place.

417. Maxwell, J. C. "Notes on Dr. Faustus." *Notes and Queries*, NS 11 (1964), 262.
Offers seven corrections and emendations to Greg's notes (30).

418. Mebane, John Spencer. "Art and Magic in Marlowe, Jonson, and Shakespeare: The Occult Tradition in *Dr. Faustus, The Alchemist,* and *The Tempest.*" *DAI*, 35 (1975), 7316A–7317A.

419. Morgan, Gerald. "Harlequin Faustus: Marlowe's Comedy of Hell." *Humanities Association Bulletin*, 18:1 (1967), 22–34.
Faustus is led through a circus of confusions and evasions to his spiritual destruction as the audience watches, as it were, like devils themselves.

420. Muir, Kenneth. "Marlowe's *Doctor Faustus.*" *Philologica Praegensia*, 9 (1966), 395–408.
Muir sees the play as a revolt against the authority of all law, civil and temporal, eternal and divine.

421. Nagarajan, S. "The Philosophy of Doctor Faustus." *Essays in Criticism,* 20 (1970), 485–487.

Reply to French (entry 379). Faustus' philosophical knowledge is not limited or impaired, as is supposed by French.

422. Nosworthy, J. M. "Coleridge on a Distant Prospect of Faust." *Essays and Studies,* 11 (1957), 69–96.

Coleridge planned a play called *Michael Scott* which he never wrote but wrote about; his remarks reveal some very acute observations about Marlowe's play.

423. O'Brien, Margaret. "Christian Belief in *Doctor Faustus.*" *English Literary History,* 37 (1970), 1–11.

In aspiring to godhead, Faustus "destroys himself by his impatience." The drama reflects Christian doctrine as expressed in Scripture and in Aquinas and Augustine, but Faustus misreads theology and finds "condemnation" instead of *caritas.* The play's brilliance rests in the concept of the mystical Body of Christ (John 15:1–7) which Marlowe inverts in the action, and "refocuses Christian values away from doctrine and codes to the heart of a personal commitment to a person, marked by fidelity." This critic believes that Marlowe's view of religion was too advanced for his audiences.

423a. Okerlund, A. N. "The Intellectual Folly of Doctor Faustus." *Studies in Philology,* 74 (1977), 258–278.

Examines the hero and the play in the context of its intellectual milieu as "a reflection of the scholastic and philosophical controversies preoccupying the literate public throughout all of contemporary Europe." Faustus abandons classical and accepted methods of obtaining truth and abrogates his intellectual and linguistic powers. Consummate intellect embodied in Marlowe's hero wilfully rejects the power to reason; Cambridge freshmen could recognize fallacies in Aristotle which Faustus could not. He is like a modern scholar in desiring to free himself of human limitations; the greatest temptation of all (278).

424. Ornstein, Robert. "The Comic Synthesis in *Doctor Faustus.*" *English Literary Renaissance,* 22 (1955), 165–172. (Reprinted in entries 28 and 33.)

Without maintaining definitely Marlowe's authorship of the comic scenes in the play, Ornstein tries to show the integrity of

comic action to the meaning of the whole play: the "measure of
his tragic fall is the amusing disparity between his apirations and
his achievements." The play depicts no tragic failure of a good
rebellion but instead exhibits "the knowledge that the Comic
Spirit hovers over the Icarian flight of the self-announced super-
man."

425. ———. "Marlowe and God: The Tragic Theology of *Doctor
  Faustus.*" *Publications of the Modern Language Association,*
  83 (1968), 1378–1385.
  Marlowe's most profound statement is *Doctor Faustus,* for
he recognized the destructiveness of superhuman power even as
he saw man attracted inevitably to transcendent will. The contradictions of the tragedy are the result of mature, sober reflection on the relationship between God and individuals.

426. Ostrowski, Witold. "The Interplay of the Subjective and Objective in Marlowe's *Dr. Faustus.*" In *Studies in Language
  and Literature in Honor of Margaret Schlauch,* ed. M.
  Bahmer, S. Helsztynski, and J. Krzyzanowski, 1966, pp.
  293–305.

427. Palmer, D. J. "Magic and Poetry in *Doctor Faustus.*" *Critical Quarterly,* 6 (1964), 56–67. (Reprinted in entry 33, 200–
  214.)
  Marlowe's ability to create illusion out of poetry is most
beautifully demonstrated by this play, for he is able to suggest
the gulf at the play's heart between idea and act, word and deed.
His language solves dramatic problems of space and time in *Doctor Faustus* and gives beauty and dignity to the damnable action.

428. Patrides, C. A. "Renaissance and Modern Views of Hell."
  Harvard Theological Review, 57 (1964), 217–236.
  Deals briefly with Marlowe's play.

429. Pearce, T. M. "Jasper Heywood and Marlowe's *Doctor
  Faustus.*" *Notes and Queries,* 197 (1952), 200–201.
  Echoes of *Thyestes* (1560; reprinted 1581) in Marlowe's
play, 11. 1422–1449 in the Tucker Brooke edition.

430. Podis, JoAnne. "The Concept of Divinity in *Doctor Faustus.*" *Theatre Annual,* 27 (1971–1972), 89–102.

Faustus believes in an Old Testament God and cannot accept because of his intellectual presumption the idea of a merciful Savior. The play, this critic claims, affirms Christian values and its scheme of redemption.

431. Politzer, Henry. "Of Time and *Dr. Faustus.*" *Monatschafte* 51 (1960), 145–155.
   Deals with Mann and the chapbook; in passing with Marlowe.

432. Ransom, Marian, Roderick Cooke, and T. M. Pearce. "'German Valdes and Cornelius' in Marlowe's *Doctor Faustus.*" *Notes and Queries,* NS 9 (1962), 329–331.
   Valdes may allude to Juan de Valdes, secretary to the Emperor Charles V, who was accused of heresy. Cornelius may be a reference to one Antoine Cornelius, a lawyer living in France at the time of Francis I, who wrote an heretical pamphlet on the state of unbaptized infants. Two heretics would be fit companions for Faustus.

433. Reed, Robert R., Jr. "Nick Bottom, Doctor Faustus, and the Ass's Head." *Notes and Queries,* NS 6 (1959), 252–254.
   Although Bottom's transformation might come from Scot's *Discoverie of Witchcraft,* a more likely source is Marlowe's play. [What happened to Apuleius' romance?]

434. Reynolds, J. A. "Faustus's Flawed Learning." *English Studies,* 57:4 (1976), 329–336.
   Faustus' "misconception of human learning" is ironic basis of the tragedy "both in its thematic implications and its dramatic form." The tragedy grows from Faustus' faulty perception of the "uses of the human mind." The thoughts about learning are not drawn from the *English Faust Book* but are Marlowe's own innovation, and perhaps draw on Greville's *Treatise on Human Learning.* The play's hero reflects a contemporary view about "the nature and purpose of human learning" whereas the *EFB* takes the traditional approach that any knowledge not leading to salvation is erroneous. Faustus confuses the spheres where the mind may best operate.

435. ———. "Marlowe's *Dr. Faustus:* 'Be a Divine in a Show' and 'When All Is Done Divinity Is Best'." *American Notes and Queries,* 13 (1975), 131–133.

No inconsistency in these lines; they are just survivals of lines from the source book.

436. Rosador, Kurt Tetzel von. "*Doctor Faustus:* 1604 und 1616." *Anglia,* 90 (1972), 470–493.

An exhaustive rehearsal of the issues for the authority of the A and B texts which recommends an eclectic approach to new editions drawing from both.

437. Sachs, Arieh. "The Religious Despair of Doctor Faustus. *Journal of English and Germanic Philology,* 63 (1964), 625–647.

Faustus' sin is a religious one; his denial of the possibility of salvation gives the play a Reformation flavor. Because he is intrigued by his ultimate fate, Faustus becomes incapable of seeking grace and being redeemed.

438. Sanders, Wilbur. "Marlowe's *Doctor Faustus.*" *Melbourne Critical Review,* 7 (1964), 78–91.

The play is ambiguous with regard to the diabolical, and the protagonist is caught in a syndrome of attraction and repulsion; indeed, so is the audience. The play potentially is a tragedy of the divided consciousness, its appeal deep, modern, and perennial.

439. Seiferth, Howard. "The Concept of the Devil and the Myth of the Pact in Literature Prior to Goethe." *Monatschafte,* 44 (1952), 271–289.

Survey of main shared characteristics with passing references to Marlowe: the Devil as accuser on Judgment Day; as tempter; as fallen angel (Contrite Devil); as pact maker; he is always associated with mechanical or scientific devices.

440. Sewall, Richard B. *The Vision of Tragedy.* New Haven and London: Yale University Press, 1959, pp. 57–67, 159–160. (Reprinted in entries 33 and 378.)

"Perhaps Marlowe believed that Faustus was doomed no matter how humble his repentance; or he may have conceived him as so hardened in his rationalism as to believe faith a mere function of reason. But the final scene gives a sense, not so much of the justice and goodness of the universe as of the transcendent human individual, caught in the consequences of a dilemma

which, granted the condions of his times, it was impossible for
any imaginative man wholly to avoid." Marlowe introduces audiences to the modern theme of the divided soul; "Faustus is tragic
because he recognized the dilemma as real."

441. Shapiro, I. A. "The Significance of a Date." *Shakespeare
Survey,* 8 (1955), 100–105.
   Questions the early date of Faustus in light of other evidence involving the hand of Anthony Mundy in *John a Kent* and
in *Sir Thomas More.*

442. Smidt, Kristian. "Two Aspects of Ambition in Elizabethan
Tragedy: *Doctor Faustus* and *Macbeth.*" *English Studies,* 50
(1969), 235–248.
   Comparative study: Faustus is a scholar "first and last,"
whose earthly ambitions are pretty much fulfilled by the devil he
conjures up, but he is not damned either for moral depravity or
ambition. The word "damned," Smidt points out, Marlowe shied
away from in his plays. He is damned for psychological reasons;
Marlowe the atheist [!] cannot provide a pious or edifying conclusion. *Doctor Faustus* is a "dialogue between ambition and futil-
ity."

443. Smith, Warren D. "The Nature of Evil in *Doctor Faustus.*"
Modern Language Review, 60 (1965), 171–175.
   Evil is revealed as "petty in nature" and its power in the
play is undermined by those displays of its alleged appeal to
Faustus.

443a. Snow, Edward A. "Marlowe's *Doctor Faustus* and the
Ends of Desire." In *Two Renaissance Mythmakers,* ed.
Alvin Kernan (see 122 and 123), pp. 70–110.
   A penetrating phenomenological approach to the play
which astutely points out the varied and contrasting uses of the
word and ideas associated with "end(s)" to show the forcefulness
of Marlowe's conception of his hero and the drama.

444. Snyder, Susan. "Marlowe's Doctor Faustus as an Inverted
Saint's Life." *Studies in Philology,* 63 (1966), 565–577.
   Play consciously inverts the patterns of action in hagiog-

raphy and thus the impact of the play is heightened by negative contrasts.

445. Steadman, John M. "Averros and Dr. Faustus: Some Additional Parallels." *Notes and Queries,* NS 9 (1962), 327–329.
    Argues that allusions in the drama to philosophical Averroism function to stress Faustus' "incompatability with Christianity."

446. ———. "Faustus and Averros." *Notes and Queries,* NS 3 (1956), 416.
    Latin source for I.iii.

447. Stroup, Thomas B. "*Doctor Faustus* and *Hamlet*: Contrasting Kinds of Christian Tragedy." *Comparative Drama,* 5 (1971), 243–253.
    Faustus' finest qualities, his "great intellect enabling great learning and both contributing to a great sensitivity of conscience—actually turn upon him and crush him by despair." The play ends with Faustus' psychomachia, whereas Hamlet opens with a similar struggle. Hamlet moves beyond despair to win. The plays exhibit two poles of Christian drama: Faustus asserts will, denies God, and is destroyed; Hamlet, forced to take up a burden, succeeds by trial and error.

448. Summers, Claude J. and Ted-Larry Pebworth. "Marlowe's *Faustus* and the Earl of Bedford's Motto." *English Language Notes,* 9 (1972), 165–167.
    In quoting "che sera sera" Marlowe's hero ignores Providence and denies Grace as rendered in contemporary literature—*cf.* Whetstone's poem on the Earl of Bedford.

449. Tanner, James T. F. "*Doctor Faustus* as Orthodox Christian Sermon." *Dickinson Review,* 2 (1969), 23–31.
    The play explicitly condemns and punishes the actions of its hero.

450. Tibi, Pierre, "*Dr. Faustus* et la cosmologie de Marlowe." *Revue des Langues Vivantes,* 40 (1974), 212–227.
    Marlowe's intellectual beliefs find support in empirical

skepticism; therefore he rejects the sphere of fire and the concept of a crystalline heaven in *Doctor Faustus.*

451. Traci, Philip. "Marlowe's Faustus as Artist: A Suggestion about the Theme of the Play." *Renaissance Papers* (1966), 3–9.
    Faustus' wants to be like Prospero but unlike Shakespeare's magician, he loses his soul in his pursuit of art and cannot break from it to re-enter humanity renewed.

452. Versefield, Martin. "Some Remarks on Marlowe's *Faustus.*" *English Studies in Africa,* 1 (1958), 134–143.
    A thoughtful essay in which the author sees the drama as having been written shortly after Marlowe came down from Cambridge; it presents the tragedy of a man who violates the fundamental hierarchical order of medieval scholasticism.

453. Walsh, Charles E. "Una M. Ellis-Fermor to W. W. Greg on The Damnation of Faustus: An Unpublished Letter." *Emporia State Research Studies,* 15 (1966), 5–7.
    Compliments Greg for his 1946 essay concerning the sin of demonality which irrevocably damns Faustus.

454. Walsh, Maureen P. "Demigod, Devil, or Man: A Reconsideration of the Character of Faustus." *Nassau Review* (Long Island), 2:1 (1970), 54–65.
    Faustus is no demigod, only a man in whom first the diabolic and then the bestial predominate and so destroy him.

455. Waswo, Richard. "Damnation, Protestant Style: Faustus, Macbeth, and Christian Tragedy." *Journal of Medieval and Renaissance Studies,* 4 (1974), 63–99.
    Points out that both tragic heroes commit sins against the Holy Ghost. In accord with the Protestant theological perception of this sin, both men as a consequence are committed to lives of misery, psychological self-imprisonment, and the inability to repent: "once the decisions are made, there is nowhere to go but down." Both plays reflect the religious preoccupations of the time.

456. Waugh, Butler. "Deep and Surface Structure in Traditional and Sophisticated Literature: Faust." *South Atlantic Bulletin*, 33: 3 (1968), 14–17.

Early post-Chomsky application of "deep" and "surface" structural concepts to Marlowe's play, yielding a further indication of how Marlowe adapted his sources for the stage. As Faustus tries to use magic to escape the human condition, its power ironically subverts his desire.

457. West, Robert H. "The Impatient Magic of Dr. Faustus." *English Literary Renaissance*, 4 (1974), 218–240.

Claims that critics ought to honor Elizabethan knowledge of magic more than they have before, thus turning Faustus into an heroic rebel. Sinning for ignoble reasons by dubious means prevents Faustus from finding a way to repent; the play does have a heroic dimension but, most important of all, a moral impact.

458. Westlund, Joseph. "The Orthodox Christian Framework of Marlowe's *Faustus*." *Studies in English Literature*, 3 (1963), 191–205.

The play is consistently realized as an orthodox Christian tragedy; Marlowe's hero acts in ways that lead to despair in a Christian context, *not* atheism.

459. Wyman, Linda. "How Plot and Subplot Unite in Marlowe's *Faustus*." *College English Association*, 37:1 (1974), 14–16.

Subplot ironically provides a prefiguration of Faustus' final punishment in the punishments upon Robin and Dick.

460. Zimansky, Curt A. "Marlowe's *Faustus*: The Date Again." *Philological Quarterly*, 41 (1962), 181–187.

In style and construction Faustus is related to the Tamburlaine plays; three allusions to works current in 1589 argue to date Marlowe's play at this time: Zimansky finds echoes in *Faustus* from Harvey, Nashe, and *A Knack to Know a Knave*.

7. THE JEW OF MALTA

461. Babb, Howard S. "Policy in Marlowe's *The Jew of Malta.*"
English Literary History, 24 (1957), 85–94.

Very important essay which observes that the word *policy,*
occurring throughout Marlowe's play, is actually used in opposing
senses. On one hand, *policy* refers to the selfish pursuit of private gain and power through unscrupulous intrigue in the conception of the stage-Machiavel; on the other hand it is used as a term
of approbation to describe the conduct of public affairs: "prudent,
expedient, or advantageous procedure." Babb implies that the
ambiguous moral perspective in the play is distilled in the uses of
the term policy in it, for even those who pay lip-service to the
positive connotations of the term practice policy in the negative
sense, like Barabas.

462. Bawcutt, N. W. "Machiavelli and Marlowe's *The Jew of
Malta.*" *Renaissance Drama,* NS 3 (1970), 3–49.

A scholarly and persuasive essay that maintains that the
use of Machiavelli's ideas in Marlowe's play do not follow a delib-
erate and exact polemic; rather, *The Jew of Malta* reflects the
habits of mind of Marlowe and his contemporaries, who made a
relative application of Machiavellian ideology in confronting topical issues. Thus, both negative and positive elements of
Machiavellian doctrine are mixed, attitudes derived from his
works on the one hand and his critics, like Gentillet, on the
other.

463. ————. "Marlowe's *The Jew of Malta* and Foxe's *Acts and
Monuments.*" *Notes and Queries,* NS 15 (1968), 250.

The undermining strategy in *The Jew of Malta,* V.v,
24–31, may be derived from Foxe's book, I, p. 754, describing an
event occurring during the Turk's seizure of Alba Regalis in Hun-
gary in 1453.

463a. Beecher, Don. "The Jew of Malta and the Ritual of the Inverted Moral Order." *Cahiers Elisabethains: Etudes sur la Pre-Renaissance et la Renaissance Anglaises*, 12 (1977), 45–58.

An interesting attempt to see the play's unity of intent in terms of mature audience response: Marlowe seeks to "revitalize through contemporary modes and idioms [of the drama] the powerful drama of the Middle Ages." Beecher claims that "beyond the prologue the play is a sermon on vice [where] morality is in the mind of the beholder both to sin and redeem himself" through the irony of inverted morality. Marlowe's drama strikes a "delicate balance" between the vicarious enjoyment of acting out evil impulses and our recognition "of the nature of evil inherent in men."

464. Breuer, Horst. "Marlowe's *Der Juda von Malta.*" *Germanisch-romanisch Monatschafte*, Neue Folge 25 (1975), 401–422.

A Marxist interpretation of the play that seeks to resolve its contraries in terms of social and economic alienation as described in *Das Kapital* and elsewhere.

465. Carpenter, Nan C. "Infinite Riches: A Note on Marlovian Unity." *Notes and Queries*, 196 (1951), 50–52.

The lust for gold in Marlowe's play unifies the action at all levels; in essence, all the characters spin variations on this theme and the play's moral is that disaster will befall all those who are motivated by their avarice.

466. Cole, Douglas. "The Comic Accomplice in Elizabethan Revenge Tragedy." *Renaissance Drama*, 9 (1966), 125–139.

The Barabas-Ithamore relationship provides an absurd parody of the genuine evil in the play. It prompts our quick intellectual response and moves the tragedy into the realm of satire.

467. D'Andrea, Antonio. "Studies on Machiavelli and His Reputation in the Sixteenth Century: Marlowe's Prologue to *The Jew of Malta.*" *Medieval and Renaissance Studies*, 5 (1961), 214–248.

468. Dessen, Allan C. "The Elizabethan Stage Jew and Christian Example: Gerontus, Barabas, and Shylock." *Modern Language Quarterly*, 35 (1974), 231–245.

All these characters serve to indict Christian society for failing to live up to its protestations of *caritas*. In Marlowe's play, Barabas's actions expose Malta, a city that is Christian in name, but not in deed.

469. Flosdorf, J. W. "The 'Odi et Amo' Theme in *The Jew of Malta*." *Notes and Queries*, NS 7 (1960), 10–14.

Argues for the unity of the play in terms of the conflict of love and hate.

470. Freeman, Arthur. "A Source for The *Jew of Malta*." *Notes and Queries*, NS - (1962), 139–141.

Detects a partial likeness between Barabas and Jonathanas in the fifteenth-century Croxton Play of the Sacrament.

471. Friedenreich, Kenneth. "*The Jew of Malta* and the Critics: A Paradigm for Marlowe Studies." *Papers on Language and Literature*, 13:3 (1977), 318–335.

A full survey of interpretations of the play in this century. The author sees the major development in criticism during this period as a shift from the disintegration thesis of Tucker Brooke and others, to a conception of the play as bitterly humorous and ironic—all Marlowe's—as expressed by T. S. Eliot and many others since. Concludes that in the course of debating these issues, the theatricality of the play has too long been overlooked.

472. Friedman, Alan Warren. "The Shackling of Accidents in Marlowe's *The Jew of Malta*." *Texas Studies in Literature and Language*, 8 (1965), 155–167.

Sees Barabas' fall resulting from "A fundamental incompatability between Barabas' vision of himself—his selfish behavioral code, not unlike a hermit's—and his vision of others." Barabas mistakenly assumes that the real threat to his possessions is the Turks, not the rapacious Christians. Barabas is seen as a hopelessly naïve man whose efforts to save his city ironically destroy him, a victim of the Christians' opportunism.

473. Harbage, Alfred. "Innocent Barabas." *Tulane Drama Review*, 8:4 (1964), 47–58 (Reprinted in entry 37.)

This critic sees the play as a savage game of Jew-baiting. His article is a stern corrective offered to those critics who argue that Marlowe's sympathies are with Barabas in the play.

474. Hunter, G. K. "The Theology of Marlowe's *The Jew of Malta.*" *Journal of the Warburg and Courtland Institutes,* 27 (1965), 211–240. (Reprinted in entry 37.)

Marlowe's audience would interpret Barabas' Judaism not as a creed but as a moral condition; Marlowe fabricates a web of ironies and inversions about the Jew in order to undermine the idea that Malta is a Christian "bulwark." His use of theology in the play is not to flaunt his personal skepticism but rather to chastize Christians by the example of Barabas.

475. Kocher, Paul H. "English Legal History in Marlowe's *Jew of Malta.*" *Huntington Library Quarterly,* 26 (1963), 155–163.

Many of those receiving alms from the Bishop of Rochester in 1529 or 1530 were killed when one Richard Rouse poisoned the porridge. Rouse was eventually boiled to death for his crime; Marlowe probably adapted this material for the actions and eventual punishment of Barabas.

476. Kreisman, Arthur. "The Jew of Marlowe and Shakespeare." *Shakespeare Newsletter,* 8 (1958), 29.

Synopsis of annual Gresham lecture. Argues that Jews in Elizabethan England, though few, enjoyed the special protection of influential and powerful persons.

477. *Marlowe's "The Jew of Malta": Grammar of Policy.* (MidM Series 1, No 2) Urbana: University of Illinois, Department of English, 19. Leonard F. Dean, "A Good Middle-Class Boy: A Note on Marlowe's Comedy," p. 1; Michael Bristol, "Elizabethan Artifice: The Theater of Duplicity," pp. 2–4; Neil Kleinman, "A Credible Stage: The Aesthetics of Politics," pp. 5–7.

Three incidental notes on the play.

478. McMillin, Scott, "The Ownership of *The Jew of Malta, Friar Bacon,* and *The Ranger's Comedy.*" *English Language Notes,* 9 (1972), 249–252.

Maintains the plays were not owned by Henslowe, but by Alleyn. Bearing on date and performance of Marlowe's play.

479. Maxwell, J. C. "How Bad Is the Text of *The Jew of Malta?*" *Modern Language Review,* 48:4 (1953), 434–438. (Reprinted in entry 37.)
    A brief but important essay that defends the integrity of the play's text despite the attempts of some to explain away comic scenes as not having been written by Marlowe. Cogently observes that "manuscripts, unlike apples, do not become corrupt simply by lying in a drawer."

480. Pearce, T. M. "Marlowe's *The Jew of Malta,* IV.vi, 7–10." *Explicator,* 9 (1951), item 40.
    Re: "Rivo" as "drunk" (Ithamore).

481. Peavy, Charles E. "*The Jew of Malta:* Anti-Semitic or Anti-Catholic?" *McNiese Review,* 11 (1959–1960), 51–60.
    The play is fundamentally anti-Catholic and anti-Papist. The surface anti-Semitism covers the far more vicious attack on the Catholic clergy and their cupidity.

482. Purcell, H. D. "Whetstone's *English Myrrour* and Marlowe's *Jew of Malta.*" *Notes and Queries,* NS 13 (1966), 288–290.
    Suggests parallels to Whetstone in Marlowe by attributing to Jews the vices of poisoning, Machiavellism, necromancy, and atheism. Barabas embodies these vices.

483. Rothstein, Eric. "Structure as Meaning in *The Jew of Malta.*" *Journal of English and Germanic Philology,* 65 (1966), 260–273.
    The play's theme is self-interest; Barabas is in turn betrayed by the three people he trusts—Abigail, Ithamore, and Ferneze—while the action of the play turns on parodies of Scripture, Renaissance ideals of friendship and parentage, even of pastoralism.

484. Rusche, H. G. "Two Proverbial Images in Whitney's *A Choice of Emblemes* and Marlowe's *The Jew of Malta.*" *Notes and Queries,* NS 11 (1964), 261.

Two images in Barabas' soliloquy (V.ii, 26–47) are indebted to Whitney's emblem book (p. 181), where there appears an image of Occasion or Fortune.

485. Schuman, Samuel. "'Occasion's Bald Behind': A Note on the Sources of an Emblematic Image in *The Jew of Malta*." *Modern Philology*, 70 (1973), 234–235.

The phrase in the play is not a classical one, but a Renaissance commonplace found in Alciati's emblem book (1531) and in Whitney's *Choice of Emblemes* (1586).

486. Segal, Eric. "Marlowe's *Schadenfreude*: Barabas as Comic Hero." In *Veins of Humor: Harvard Studies in English No. 3*, Harry Levin, ed. Cambridge, Massachusetts: Harvard University Press, 1972, pp. 69–92.

Play's appeal, and that especially of Barabas, is based on the audience's enjoyment of watching others get hurt. The instinct for this kind of comedy is as old as Aristophanes and as recent as slapstick; its appeal is deeply rooted in our subconscious.

487. Simmons, J. L. "Elizabethan Stage Practice and Marlowe's *The Jew of Malta*." *Renaissance Drama*, NS 4 (1971), 93–104.

Argues that the area around the protruding stage of the Elizabethan public theater was used in performance of scenes like that of the throwing of Barabas from Malta's city walls.

488. Smith, James L. "*The Jew of Malta* in the Theatre." In *Christopher Marlowe*, pp. 3–23 Brian Morris, ed. (See entry 170.)

An intelligent survey of performance practice of the play which emphasizes its inherent theatricality, despite the limited expectations placed on the play by most Marlowe scholars in "the study."

489. Spivack, Bernard. *Shakespeare and the Allegory of Evil*. New York: Columbia University Press, 1959. See pp. 346–353 on *The Jew of Malta*.

Argues that Marlowe's play is patriotic and Christian, but that in Barabas Marlowe transforms the Vice figure into one with tragic potential and proportions.

490. Sternlicht, Sanford. "The Iterative Sun Images in Marlowe's Plays." *English Record*, 18:2 (1967), 28–35. (See also entry 560.)
    In this paper, *The Jew of Malta* is noteworthy in that it is Marlowe's only drama that does not rely on iterative sun imagery; Sternlicht suggests that its over-use in the other plays may be a sign of dramatic weakness.

491. Susman, Maxine S. "Interpretations of Jewish Character in Renaissance and Recent Literature." *DAI*, 35 (1974), 1063A. (Cornell University)

492. Welsh, Robert Ford. "Evidence of Heywood Spellings in *The Jew of Malta.*" *Renaissance Papers*, (1963), 3–9.
    Evidence of spelling errors by Heywood weakens the case that he revised the play at all.

493. Willbern, David P. "The Elizabethan Revenge Play: A Psychoanalytic Study." *DAI*, 34 (1973), 1261A. (University of California, Berkeley)

494. Woodson, William C. "Elizabethan Villains and the Seared Conscience: The Application of a Theological Concept to Suggest the Credibility of Barabas, Aaron, Richard III, and Iago." *DAI*, 30 (1969), 1154A–1155A. (University of Pennsylvania)

495. Zitt, Hersch L. "The Jew in the Elizabethan World Picture." *Historia Judaica*, 14 (1952), 53–60.
    A general account of attitudes; Zitt believes Elizabethans saw the Jews in one sense as beneath the Third Order of creation (Men) for their murder of Christ, but also above the Fourth Order (Animals) because they were capable of being converted to Christianity. Incidental reference to Barabas and to Shylock.

8. THE MASSACRE AT PARIS

496. Galloway, David. "The Ramus Scene in Marlowe's *The Massacre at Paris.*" *Notes and Queries*, 198 (1953), 146–147.
    The Ramus scene provides a pause in the middle of the play's "bloody action" that is intended to heighten dramatic tension.

497. Glenn, John R. "The Martyrdom of Ramus in Marlowe's *The Massacre at Paris.*" *Papers on Language and Literature*, 9 (1973), 365–379.
    The Ramus murder is used by Marlowe as a focal point in the thrust of counter-Reformation activities and Protestant opportunism depicted in this bleak Play. Ramus embodies humane values which he defends against political and religious extremism. His historicity adds force to his murder scene.

498. Oliver, H. J. "Marlowe's *Massacre at Paris.*" *TLS*, 11 November, 1965, p. 1003.
    William Oxbury did not edit the play, though many later editors assume or imply that he did.

9. TAMBURLAINE THE GREAT

499. Aggeler, A. G. "Marlowe and the Development of Tragical
    Satire." *English Studies*, 58:3 (1977), 209–220.
    Marlowe points the way towards Jacobean theatrical taste
in his use of satire, which ironically offsets his tragic heroes' actions. Aggeler concentrates on the rhetoric in *2 Tamburlaine*
which tends to demolish Tamburlaine rather than glorify him. His
destruction of Calyphas "provides a ghastly vindication of his
[Marlowe's] satiric perception that Tamburlaine's aspiration is
self-destructive and unnatural."

500. Anderson, Donald K. "Tamburlaine's 'Perpendicular' and
    the T-in-O Maps." *Notes and Queries*, NS 21 (1974), 284–
    286.
    Explains reference in *1 Tamburlaine* (IV.iv, 83–84) in
terms of medieval cartography and makes Damascus, not
Jerusalem, the "centre of the world."

501. Armstrong, William A. "The Enigmatic Elizabethan Stage."
    English, 13 (1961), 216–220.
    Notes I.iii. in *2 Tamburlaine* may suggest that a tentlike
structure was used on the Elizabethan public stage for interior
scenes.

502. ———. *"Tamburlaine* and the *Wounds of Civil War."* *Notes
    and Queries*, NS 5 (1958), 381–383.
    Argues that *Tamburlaine* was written first and that Lodge's
play was written to "provide the Admiral's Men with an acceptable variation of the theme of the conqueror." Scilla, unlike Marlowe's hero, retires from the world; Lodge's "titan" turns into a
"stoic philosopher."

503. Barber, C. L. "The Death of Zenocrate: 'Conceiving and
    Subduing Both'." *Literature and Psychology*, 16 (1966),
    15–24.

Deals with psychological ramifications of Tamburlaine's actions in Part II, where he embalms Zenocrate's corpse in gold, burns the city where she died, and carries her mummy around with him. Barber sees Tamburlaine attempting overcome the fear of his own mortality. See also Norman Holland's Comment following Barber's article, pp. 25–26, which identifies Marlowe as an "oral" personality, because hunger (for power, knowledge, wealth) is the chief theme in his plays.

504. Battenhouse, Roy W. *Marlowe's Tamburlaine: A Study in Renaissance Moral Philosophy.* Nashville: Vanderbilt University Press, 1964. A reprint, with corrections, of the 1941 original.

Perhaps the single most important argument for Marlowe's political and religious orthodoxy in our century. Battenhouse marshals much secondary evidence to show that Marlowe conceived of his Scythian hero as tragic, doomed to fail because of his ambition and his godlessness. He is "God's Scourge" but eventually forgets himself; the play is a ten-act "moral tragedy." Battenhouse's book is an excellent piece of research that shows the possibilities and the pitfalls of historical criticism.

505. ———. "Protestant Apologetics and the Subplot of 2 Tamburlaine." *English Literary Renaissance*, 3 (1973), 30–43.

Following earlier authors, Marlowe shows Sigismund breaking faith in order to show his audiences that perjury by Christian princes will be punished by God. As perjury is closely related to blasphemy, the episode foreshadows Tamburlaine's eventual destruction when, as scourge, he dares God out of his heaven.

506. ———. "The Relation of Henry V to Tamburlaine." *Shakespeare Survey*, 27 (1974), 71–79.

Critics have long noted the similarities between the two plays, but have not enumerated in detail what these are: both imitate the sun; both perform exploits on horseback; both use threatening language and commit atrocities (though Tamburlaine commits more); both perform blood ceremonials; and both destroy for their reputations—Tamburlaine kills Calyphas while Henry "kills" Falstaff by rejecting him. Shakespeare's play is a "critique of antique dreams of heroism" in showing that even the superheroes are unable to "resist decline into social chaos."

507. Beck, Ervin. "Tamburlaine for the Modern Stage." *Educational Theatre Journal*, 23 (1971), 62–74.
   An account of modern stage practices and productions.

508. Benaquist, Lawrence M. "The Ethical Structure of *Tamburlaine*, Part I." *Thoth*, 10:2 (1969), 3–19.
   The play's action reiterates Tamburlaine's greatness as warrior and hero through one display of power after another; despite the audience's initial hesitation to accept him, by the end of the drama they approve deeds they might otherwise abhor.

509. ————. "The Tripartite Structure of Marlowe's Tamburlaine Plays and *Edward II*." *DAI*, 31 (1971), 6003A. (Syracuse University)

510. ————. *The Tripartite Structure of Marlowe's Tamburlaine Plays and Edward II*. (Elizabethan and Renaissance Studies, No. 43) James Hogg, ed. Salzburg: Institut für Englische Sprache und Literatur, 1975. 220 pp.
   Repetition of incident, long thought a defect in *Tamburlaine*, is actually the way in which Marlowe sets up and then systematically debases his hero in the two parts of the play. Part I takes an unpopular historical figure and makes him unbelievably powerful and successful; in Part II he declines, recovering his grandeur only in death: "But it is also true that Tamburlaine does not achieve what he set out to achieve, and what he essentially died for: the immortality of his empire. After the eulogies are completed, Callepine still waits nearby" (p. 121).

511. Blau, Herbert. "Language and Structure in Poetic Drama." *Modern Language Quarterly*, 18 (1957), 27–34.
   Passing reference to *1 Tamburlaine* for illustration.

512. Boas, Guy. "*Tamburlaine* and the Horrific." *English*, 8 (1951), 275–277.
   Marlowe's play as staged by Tyrone Guthrie reiterates the lesson taught the world by Hitler.

513. Brooks, Charles. "*Tamburlaine* and Attitudes towards Women." *English Literary History*, 24 (1957), 1–11.
   Erotic, courtly, romantic, and conventionally moral attitudes are expressed in *Tamburlaine*, "but they do not illustrate

a simple code" of behavior. Courtship in the plays is seen as a competition whose end is conquest, and thus analogous to Tamburlaine's imposition of order on the world by force of arms—the world in conflicts of war and love "proclaims the nobility of will" in Marlowe's plays.

514. Brown, William J. "Chapman as Marlowe's Poetic Successor: *Hero and Leander* (III, 183–198) and 2 *Tamburlaine*, I.iv." *Journal of the Illinois Speech and Theatre Association*, 29 (1975), 27–31.

Marlowe's play is echoed by analogy in Chapman's continuation of *Hero and Leander*. "Chapman, I suggest, derives his portrait of Marlowe by borrowing and adapting the climactic image from 2 *Tamburlaine*, I.iv., wherein emphasis falls upon the idea of succession—an emphasis also primary throughout Chapman's invocation" (p. 29). Brown suggests Marlowe may have actually requested that Chapman finish his work, though proof is not conclusive.

515. ———. "Marlowe's Debasement of Bajazeth: Foxe's *Actes and Monuments* and *Tamburlaine, Part I.*" *Renaissance Quarterly*, 24 (1971), 38–48.

Points out the importance of Foxe as a source for Marlowe's play, as well as showing how Marlowe radically debases Bajazeth, the Turkish Sultan, whose treatment of Christians sets him up for defeat, humiliation, and death at the hands of Marlowe's conqueror.

516. Crockcroft, Robert. "Emblematic Irony: Some Possible Significances of Tamburlaine's Chariot." *Renaissance and Modern Studies*, 12 (1968), 33–55.

Traces Renaissance and Medieval sources of dramatic emblems in the play to suggest that Marlowe's use of the chariot ironically condemns ambition; that the replacement of lions by kings in 1 *Tamburlaine* shows the moral stature of those against their will to tyrants.

517. Cutts, John P. " 'As Fierce as Achilles Was'." *Comparative Drama*, 1 (1967), 105–109.

Cutts claims that Marlowe's play is greatly indebted to classical sources, not merely for decorative purposes, but also to intensify and extend meaning. He feels the Achilles reference (*1*

T, II.i, 77–80) ironically indicates that Tamburlaine is a coward, effete, and without nerve. In the original story to which Marlowe alludes, Achilles was disguised as a woman.

518. ————. "The Ultimate Source of Tamburlaine's White, Red, and Black Death?" *Notes and Queries*, NS 5 (1958), 146–147.

Argues for Revelations 6:2–8 as the source of the description in *1 Tamburlaine*, IV.i, 111–122.

519. Daiches, David. "Language and Action in Marlowe's *Tamburlaine*." In *More Literary Essays*. Edinburgh: Oliver & Boyd, 1968, pp. 42–69. (Reprinted in entry 43.)

Poetry in this play does not merely interpret action but embodies it: "*Tamburlaine* is a play in which the virtuosity of the actor is more important than the moral nature of his actions. The hero tells us what he is going to do before he does it; tells us what he is doing when he is doing it, and after he is done he tells us what he has done—and all in language whose grandiloquence makes almost every speech a ritual of aspiration."

520. D'Andrea, Antonio. "The Aspiring Mind: A Study of the Machiavellian Element in Marlowe's *Tamburlaine*." *Yearbook of Italian Studies*, (1972), 51–77.

The Prince affords Marlowe with the "idealogical justification for the plot of the play . . . for the character of the protagonist, and for a new dramatic style . . ." (60). D'Andrea also shows how Tamburlaine's virtues as a general and soldier derive from Machiavelli's *The Art of War*, which first appeared in English in 1562. Marlowe's complex image of Tamburlaine is also influenced by Seneca's Herculean hero.

521. Egan, Robert. "A Muse of Fire: *Henry V* in the Light of *Tamburlaine*." *Modern Language Quarterly*, 29 (1968), 15–28.

Henry V follows *Tamburlaine* in dramatic method by subordinating all characterization and plot to the central figure; they differ in the recognition by Henry of his mortality in Christian terms.

522. Fabian, Bernard. "Cynthia in the O.E.D." *Notes and Queries*, NS 6 (1959), 356.

Earliest astrological reference to Cynthia given is Milton; whereas it should be *1 Tamburlaine*, I.i, 20–23.

523. Feasey, Lynette and Evelyn. "Marlowe and the Christian Humanists." *Notes and Queries*, 196 (1951), 266–268.

"Even in *Tamburlaine* there are signs that Marlowe was well on the way to [a] reintegration of humanism and religious faith." Proofs are seen in the parallels between those passages describing Zenocrate and those "freely drawn upon in the description of Divine Wisdom in the Wisdom literature of the Bible and the Apocrypha. . . ."

524. ———. "Marlowe and the Commination Service." *Notes and Queries*, 195 (1950), 156–160.

Suggest that echoes of the Commination, also known as the Denouncing of God's Anger against Sinners, found in the Book of Common Prayer, is found in *1 Tamburlaine*, V.i. and V.ii. and in *2 Tamburlaine* in the Orcanes-Sigismund episode, II.i–iii.

525. ———. "Marlowe and the Homilies." *Notes and Queries*, 195 (1950), 7–10.

Show that source of Tamburlaine's speech in Part I at IV.i, 146–148 is modeled on the Anglican Church's *Homilies against Wilful Rebellion*, and that the source of some of Calyphas' typically scornful remarks in Part II are contained in "A Homily Against Idleness."

526. ———. "Marlowe and the Prophetic Dooms." *Notes and Queries*, 195 (1950), 356–359, 404–407, 419–421.

Discussion of imagery and incident in passages in the Tamburlaine plays with reference to Scripture and the "Biblical literature of Judgement" current at the time of the plays' run.

527. Fieler, Frank B. *Tamburlaine, Part I, and Its Audience*. (University of Florida Monographs in the Humanities, No. 8) Gainesville: University of Florida Press, 1962.

A pioneering pamphlet that discusses in detail Marlowe's manipulation of audience sympathies to Tamburlaine, whose abhorrent actions that spectator is apt to be drawn into admiring.

528. Fisher, B. P. "'Phyteus' in Marlowe's *Tamburlaine*." *Notes and Queries*, NS 22 (1975), 247–248.

Traces the allusion at V.iii, 237 in Part II to Hesychius'
Lexicon, edited in 1514 by Marcus Mursus, and available at
Cambridge throughout the century in many Continental editions.

529. Friedenreich, Kenneth. "Directions in Tamburlaine Criticism." In *Christopher Marlowe's Tamburlaine Part and Part
II*, pp. 341–352. Irving Ribner, ed. (See entry 43.)
  A survey of the principal critical trends in modern criticism of the play.

530. ———. "'Huge greatness overthrowne': The Fall of the
Empire in Marlowe's Tamburlaine Plays." *Clio* [Wisconsin],
1:2 (1972), 37–48.
  Marlowe's principal sources suggest how quickly Tamburlaine's empire fell apart after his death. While there is some indication in Part I that Marlowe was aware of this fact, he develops it fully in Part II, first, in Tamburlaine's obsession with the
future of his "empery" and ironically in the character of Calyphas,
who embodies the failure of Tamburlaine's progeny to maintain
the realms.

531. ———. "'You talks brave and bold': The Origins of an
Elizabethan Stage Device." *Comparative Drama*, 8:3 (1974),
239–253.
  Argues that the public confrontation scenes in Marlowe's
play, and in English historical plays generally, have their origins
in medieval mystery plays, St. George Mummers' Plays, and
early English poetry.

532. Gilbert, Allan. "Tamburlaine's 'Pampered Jades'." *Rivista di
Letteratura Moderne*, 4 (1954), 208–210.
  Source is from Lucan or Diodorus Siculus.

533. Guthrie, Tyrone. "*Tamburlaine*, and What It Takes."
Theatre Arts, 40 (1956), 21–23, 84–86.
  Discussion of his famous production.

534. Hookham, Hilda. *Tamburlaine the Conqueror*. London:
Hodder and Stoughton, 1962. 384 pp.
  A colorful biography of the historical figure dramatized by
Marlowe.

535. Howe, James Robinson. *Marlowe, Tamburlaine, and Magic.*
Athens, Ohio: Ohio University Press, 1976. vi + 214 pp.
    Howe's interesting approach to Marlowe's heroes is based
on the elucidation of Hermetic philosophy—embracing as it does
Neo-Platonism, magic, alchemy, astrology—and embodied in the
work of Giordano Bruno, Marlowe's contemporary. His thesis in-
volves attempting to define the inner quality of Tamburlaine and
Marlowe's other heroes in order to see from where their *energia*
comes. He sees Marlowe's figures reaching towards the attainment of semi-divinity in a Hermetic sense, though he fortunately
does not try to maintain that Marlowe's beliefs are all rooted in
Hermetic philosophy as it was understood in England at the end
of the sixteenth century.

536. Hunter, G. K. *"The Wars of Cyrus* and *Tamburlaine."*
Notes and Queries, NS 8 (1961), 395–396.
    Points out similarities between Tamburlaine and the
anonymous play which raise some new questions: was an original
play, dating from much earlier than Marlowe's, revised following
its success? Has the text of *Cyrus* been set down by a pirate
whose head was full of Marlovian phrases?

537. Jacquot, Jean. "La pensée de Marlowe dans *Tamburlaine
the Great." Études Anglaises,* 6 (1953), 322–345. [In French]
    Marlowe's ideas about Tamburlaine evolve through the
work; the work is a dramatic poem which displays an absence of
compassion and tragic feeling and thus poses grave questions
about our response to the violent deeds of the hero. Marlowe
makes us confront the truth about our fascination with tyrants and
tyranny.

538. Kaplan, Joel H. "Middleton's Tamburlaine." *Modern Language Notes,* 13:4 (1976), 258–260.
    Offers a corrective to Battenhouse, claiming that Tambur-
laine, to all Renaissance Englishmen, was ambitious in the extreme. In Middleton's *Triumph of Integrity,* Tamburlaine is
shown to be a great nobleman.

539. Khattab, E. "Muhammed in Marlowe's *Tamburlaine." University of Riyad Bulletin of the Faculty Arts* (Saudi Arabia),
1 (1970), 41–52.

540. Kimbrough, Robert. "*Tamburlaine:* A Speaking Picture in a Tragic *Glass.*" *Renaissance Drama,* 7 (1964), 20–34. (Reprinted in entry 43, pp. 282–297.)
   Anti-romantic interpretation of the first play; Marlowe is not using his hero for propaganda; he is a dramatic artist who "demonstrated a consummate skill in exercising his audience's potential aesthetic strength while he satisfied its basic desire to be entertained" (p. 20); Marlowe succeeds in dramatizing very unmalleable materials and treats ambiguity "with objectivity instead of as a sermon *exemplum.*" His prologue announces a new kind of thought-provoking drama, which his composition bears out.

541. Leech, Clifford. "The Structure of *Tamburlaine.*" *Tulane Drama Review,* 8:4 (1964), 32–46. (Reprinted in entry 43, pp. 267–281.)
   Leech sees Part I as possessing a clearly defined structure; each scene pits a character with a peculiar attribute against Tamburlaine, who overmasters them. However, each victory for the hero is seen in an increasingly unfavorable light. In Part II, Tamburlaine's actions to magnify his greatness form the basis of the play's structure, but here the contrasting elements diminish his stature.

542. LePage, Peter V. "The Search for Godhead in Marlowe's *Tamburlaine.*" *College English,* 26 (1964), 604–609.
   Interprets the play's central theme as stated in his title; LePage sees Tamburlaine's actions leading not to divinity, but to inhumanity.

543. Leslie, Nancy T. "Tamburlaine in the Theater: Tartar, Grand Guignol, or Janus?" *Renaissance Drama,* NS 4 (1971), 105–120.
   An informative and perceptive record of productions of the plays from 1919 through 1966; acknowledges the tendencies to depict or emphasize spectacle and brutality in modern productions.

544. Lever, Katherine. "The Image of Man in *Tamburlaine, Part I.*" *Philological Quarterly,* 35 (1956), 421–427.
   Play raises questions about man's nature in terms of Tam-

burlaine's behavior in different roles—as shepherd, lord, king, emperor. He violates our expectations of these roles and hence the play centers on a conflict between reality and illusion. "Tamburlaine, and through him, Man, is an enigma... [who leaves] contradictory impressions unresolved."

545. Liu, J. Y. "The Interpretation of Three Lines in Marlowe's *Tamburlaine*, Part I." *Notes and Queries*, 195 (1950), 137–138.

V.ii, 121–123 of Part I interpreted: "That which has calmed the rage of the Gods [i.e., Jove] and made them [or him] come down from heaven to feel the lovely warmth of human passion."

546. ———. "A Marlowe-Shakespearean Image Cluster." *Notes and Queries*, 196 (1951), 336–337.

The cluster is "book-love-bookbinding" found in *1 Tamburlaine* and *The Massacre at Paris,* and in Shakespeare's *Love's Labour's Lost* and *Romeo and Juliet.*

547. ———. "The Name of the Arabian King in Marlowe's *Tamburlaine.*" *Notes and Queries*, 195 (1950), 10.

The name of the king (*1 T*, V.ii, 316–317) is actually mentioned earlier in the play (I.ii, 78–79); he is called Alcidamus.

548. Lyons, Kathleen V. "Marlowe's *Tamburlaine:* A 'Tragicke Glasse'." *DAI*, 32 (1971), 925A. (Fordham University)

549. McCullen, Joseph T. "The Use of Parlor and Tavern Games in Elizabethan and Jacobean Drama." *Modern Language Quarterly*, 14 (1953), 7–14.

Refers to the card game played by Calyphas in Part II.

549a. Martin, Richard A. "Marlowe's *Tamburlaine* and the Language of Romance." *Publications of the Modern Language Association*, 93:2 (1978), 248–64.

Each play attempts to define itself as romance inasmuch as Marlowe's language asserts the "mastery of the imagination over the material world." In Part I, Tamburlaine's mastery is complete; there are no tragic realities associated with human concern in a familiar sense, for he has "the freedom to transcend the

realistic limitations of a problematic and imperfect humanity"
(258). In Part II, "Tamburlaine's death is tragic... insofar as it
manifests the subordination of the romantic imagination to necessity and reality." In this play the world of romance must "admit a
measure of defeat" (263).

550. Maxwell, J. C. "*Tamburlaine,* Part I, IV.iv, 77–79." *Notes
and Queries,* 197 (1952), 444.
        Tamburlaine's tripartite division of the world is traditional,
with references to Europe, Asia, and Africa, and does not anach-
ronistically suppose the conqueror's awareness of the New World.

551. Merchant, W. Moelwyn. "Marlowe the Orthodox." In
Christopher Marlowe, pp. 177–192. Brian Morris, ed. (See
entry 170.)
        Emphasis on *Tamburlaine* but deals with other plays as
well. Merchant claims that no orthodoxy—social, political,
religious—is purely monolithic and inviolable, "that there are
ambiguities and imponderables in the structure of orthodoxy itself." He criticizes those critics who have forgotten that "Marlowe's highly exploratory intelligence has frequently been over-
shadowed by the wilfulness of his expression and the alleged ir-
regularity of his life" (p. 181). In *Tamburlaine,* Merchant examines the conflict between Renaissance *virtu* and the moral order.

552. Moose, Roy Clifton. "A Study of Marlowe's Dramaturgy,
with Special Reference to the Structure of *Tamburlaine,
Part II.*" *DAI,* 27 (1966), 185A. (University of North
Carolina)

553. Nathanson, Leonard. "Tamburlaine's 'Pampered Jades' and
Gascoigne." *Notes and Queries,* NS 5 (1958), 53–54.
        Contends the opening four lines of IV.iii. in Part II come
from Gascoigne's *The Steele Glas* (1576): "But such as have their
stables ful yfraught / With pampered Jades, ought therewithal to
wey...." See entry 532 for a different view.

554. Nelson, T. G. A. "Marlowe and His Audience: A Study of
Tamburlaine." *Southern Review* [Adelaide, Australia], 3
(1960), 249–263.

Orthodox beliefs in Fate and Justice are shattered by Tamburlaine, who triumphs over all preconceived limitations and accepted notions of behavior in war and peace.

555. Nosworthy, J. M. "The Shakespearean Heroic Vaunt." *Review of English Studies*, 2 (1951), 259–261.
Derives from *Tamburlaine*, Part I.

556. O'Connor, John J. "Another Human Footstool." *Notes and Queries*, NS 2 (1955), 332.
Prior to Marlowe's play, readers familiar with the romance, *The History of Gerileon of England*, published in 1578 and again in 1583 and 1593, would note that Menoleris' treatment of Nabat was that which Tamburlaine meted out to Bajazeth.

557. Parr, Johnstone. *Tamburlaine's Malady and other Essays on Astrology in Elizabethan Literature*. Auburn, Alabama: University of Alabama Press, 1953.
Argues, following Camden (1929), that Tamburlaine's disposition is choleric; Parr traces its cause to the hero's stars, and the course of his career to astrology. Reviewed in *Notes and Queries*, NS 1 (1954), 181–182.

558. Pearce, T. M. "Marlowe and Castiglione." *Modern Language Quarterly*, 12 (1951), 3–12.
Tamburlaine seen in terms of models of behavior found in the great courtesy book of the sixteenth century, *The Courtier*.

559. ———. "Tamburlaine's 'Discipline to his three sonnes': An Interpretation of *Tamburlaine, Part II*." *Modern Language Quarterly*, 15 (1954), 18–27.
Sees the play in terms of its relationship to the educational ideals of Ascham and Elyot. He believes that Marlowe's interest in education of future rulers in the drama is a reply to Gosson's attack on the stage.

560. Peet, Donald. "The Rhetoric of *Tamburlaine*." *English Literary History*, 26 (1959), 137–155.
Analysis of rhetorical figures in the play (Part I) to demonstrate that through "a bold application of the tools of rhetoric to

the materials of a dramatist," Marlowe can provide continual as-
tonishment that "magnifies the importance of his hero and the
fabulous adventures of his hero, whether they are deeds of valor
or of savagery."

561. Quinn, Michael. "The Freedom of *Tamburlaine.*" *Modern
Language Quarterly*, 21 (1961), 315–320.
    As a hero Tamburlaine is unique in his ability to live up to
his own aspirations and to effect the actions that he announces in
his speeches.

562. Rais, Mahmoud. "The Representation of the Turk in English
Renaissance Drama." *DAI*, 34 (1973), 1252A–1253A. (Cornell University)

563. Ribner, Irving. "The Idea of History in Marlowe's *Tamburlaine.*" *English Literary History*, 20 (1953), 251–266.
    An important article that shows the way that Marlowe's
conception of his hero is based upon a classical view of history
rather than a Christian and providential one. The emphasis and
the subsequent audience reaction to Tamburlaine is on the individual assertion of will and *virtù*, the wooing of fortune in a
Machiavellian sense, not on the hierarchical and orderly view of
history that sees God's will guiding and vindicated in human actions. (Reprinted in R. J. Kaufmann, ed. *Elizabethan Drama:
Modern Essays in Criticism.* New York: Oxford U. Press.)

564. ———. "*Tamburlaine* and *The Wars of Cyrus.*" *Journal of
English and Germanic Philology*, 53 (1954), 569–573.
    Claims that *The Wars of Cyrus* was hurriedly printed after
the success of Marlowe's play, to corner a piece of the market in
heroic drama.

565. Richards, Susan. "Marlowe's *Tamburlaine II:* A Drama of
Death." *Modern Language Quarterly*, 26 (1965), 375–387.
(Reprinted in entry 43, pp. 298–311.)
    The play's action is permeated by death, and Tamburlaine
is its mortal agent: Tamburlaine's death, she claims, is "basically
melodramatic: he seeks to conquer death physically by fighting it
off; he then considers himself not as dying but as going to rule in
a better place;... and, finally, he seeks to ignore it by regarding

himself as still living in his sons." By refusing to acknowledge human limitations, *Tamburlaine* misses the tragic mark for the hero's "final refusal of self-knowledge" that Marlowe successfully depicts in Faustus.

566. Rickey, Mary E. "Astronomical Imagery in *Tamburlaine*." *Renaissance Papers*, (1954), pp. 63–70.
Shows how the imagery is not decorative, but related to the rise and decline of Tamburlaine's career.

567. Ross, Aden. "Tragedy of the Absurd: Marlowe's *Tamburlaine* and Camus' *Caligula*." *Thoth*, 13:2 (1973), 3–9.
A short comparative study of two leaders who unleashed a reign of unbridled terror over their subjects in mad pursuit of absolute mastery.

568. Schuster, Erika and Horst Oppel. "Die Bankett Szene in Marlowe's *Tamburlaine*." *Anglia*, 77 (1959), 340–345. [In German]
Emblematic and thematic import of the structure of the two plays: in Part I, at the feast, Tamburlaine blasphemes the Gods. In Part II, at a moment of greater triumph, this blaspheming is repeated and leads to Tamburlaine's death.

569. Smith, Warren D. "The Substance of Meaning in *Tamburlaine, Part I*." *Studies in Philology*, 67 (1970), 156–166.
Tamburlaine is not amoral nor bloodthirsty. Rather, Smith claims that the character develops consistently through the drama, resolving within himself the conflict between Mars and Venus, and achieves fulfillment in the great speech in V.ii, 69–127.

570. Sternlicht, Sanford. "Tamburlaine and the Iterative Sun-Image." *English Record*, 16 (1966), 23–29.
Marlowe employs solar imagery to mark the career of Tamburlaine as it rises, increasing in light and power and majesty. (See also entry 490.)

571. Summers, Claude J. "Tamburlaine's Opponents and Machiavelli's *Prince*." *English Language Notes*, 11 (1974), 256–258.

The successive rulers who are subdued by Tamburlaine in Part I follow Machiavelli's hierarchy of political orders from a hereditary prince (Mycetes) to a usurping one (Cosroe) to a conquering prince (Bajazeth), and finally to authoritarian, non-hereditary rulers like the Soldan. The sequence may show that Marlowe consulted Machiavelli.

572. Taylor, Robert T. "Maximinus and Tamburlaine." *Notes and Queries*, NS 4 (1957), 417–418.
Parallel between Marlowe's play and Machiavelli's description in *Il Principe* of the Roman emperor Caesar Julius Maximinus (235–238AD). Both Tamburlaine and the Roman were shepherds who deprived weak and effeminate princes of their crowns.

572a. Tennenhouse, Leonard "Baalam and Saul in the World of *II Tamburlaine*." *Neuphilologische Mitteilungen*, 78 (1977), 115–117.

573. Thomson, J. Oliver. "Marlowe's 'River Araris'." *Modern Language Review*, 48 (1953), 423–424.
Marlowe's geography at II.i, 63–67 is an example of poetic license; Marlowe was not always as scrupulous with detail as others (Ethel Seaton most notably [1924 and above, 209]) believe.

573a. Truchet, Sibyl. "*Tamburlaine* on the Modern Stage." *Cahiers Elisabethains: Etudes sur la Pre-Renaissance et la Renaissance Anglaises*, 13 (1978), 53–60.
A re-evaluation of the production of Marlowe's play, directed by Peter Hall, which opened the Olivier Theatre in London in 1976.

574. Turner, Robert Y. "Shakespeare and the Public Confrontation Scene in Early History Plays." *Modern Philology*, 62 (1964), 1–12.
An important essay showing how Shakespeare used the scene where adversaries out-vaunt each other in hierarchical order, from highest ranking individual to servants, prior to battle in order to increase dramatic tension and to set the value of the ensuing defeat or victory for the audience. Deals with *Tamburlaine* in this context. (See also entry 521.)

575. Vaughan, David Kirk. "Marlowe's Orators: Concepts of Tudor Humanist Eloquence in I and II *Tamburlaine, The Jew of Malta,* and *Doctor Faustus.*" *DAI,* 35 (1975), 4461A.

576. Velz, John W. "Episodic Structure in Four Tudor Plays: A Virtue of Necessity." *Comparative Drama,* 6 (1972), 87–102.

Pursues implications of Bevington's structural analysis of Elizabethan plays (entry 66); and sees *1 Tamburlaine* as using this structure on the one hand to aggrandize the hero's stature and on the other hand to remind the audience of his finite mortality. We see Tamburlaine capable of causing death, but incapable of preventing it, as, for instance, Zenocrate's or his own.

577. Waith, Eugene M. "Marlowe and the Jades of Asia." *Studies in English Literature,* 5 (1965), 229–245.

Beginning with a discussion of Marlowe's plays as a whole, Waith argues that in sum they are balanced works of art, not mere sounding boards for their creator's opinions. Marlowe reveals his attitudes towards his characters and also manipulates our responses to them. He is thus not lacking in the objective vision as prevailing critical opinion maintains.

578. Watson-Williams, Helen. "The Power of Words: A Reading of *Tamburlaine the Great,* Part One." *English,* 22 (1973), 13–18.

The play explores the poetic treatment and the rhetorical purposes of language as weapons, as substitutes for action, and to express "the attitude" towards human domination or the "heroic ideal." Language transforms brutal acts into things which are admirable.

579. Wehling, Mary Mellen. "Marlowe's Mnemonic Nominology, with Especial Reference to *Tamburlaine.*" *Modern Language Notes,* 78 (1958), 243–247.

Names are remarkably appropriate to their bearers; what is evident in Tamburlaine is repeated in *Edward II* and in *The Jew of Malta* as well.

580. Whitworth, Charles W. "*The Wounds of Civil War* and *Tamburlaine:* Lodge's Alleged Imitation." *Notes and Queries,* 22 (1975), 245–247.

Restates the early opinion of Paradise that on the strength of internal evidence, i.e., stagecraft and language, Lodge's play is not a poor imitation of Marlowe's but that *Tamburlaine* represents a far superior attempt in a mode tried first by Lodge.

580a. Wiedner, Elsie M. "Claudel's Overreacher: *Tête d'Or* and Marlowe's *Tamburlaine* Plays." *Claudel Studies,* 4:2 (1977), 60–70.

Compares the structure of Claudel's work to the episodic one in Marlowe's dramas; notes parallels in Act III of 2 *Tamburlaine* to Claudel. Like Marlowe, Claudel celebrates a love of power and glory in his early work (1894), but unlike his predecessor, glorification of the world is only prelude to renunciation of it: Claudel's love of power ultimately gives way to profound religious orthodoxy whereas Marlowe's vision culminates in the cosmic disillusionment of Faustus.

581. Wyler, Siegfried. "Marlowe's Technique of Communicating with His Audience as Seen in His *Tamburlaine, Part I.*" *English Studies,* 48 (1967), 306–316.

A linguistic analysis of the play based on B. L. Joseph's notion of pre-arranged codes which are established and developed between audience and dramatist during acted performances (*cf.* Joseph's *Elizabethan Acting,* 1964).

AUTHOR INDEX
[by entry number]

68881

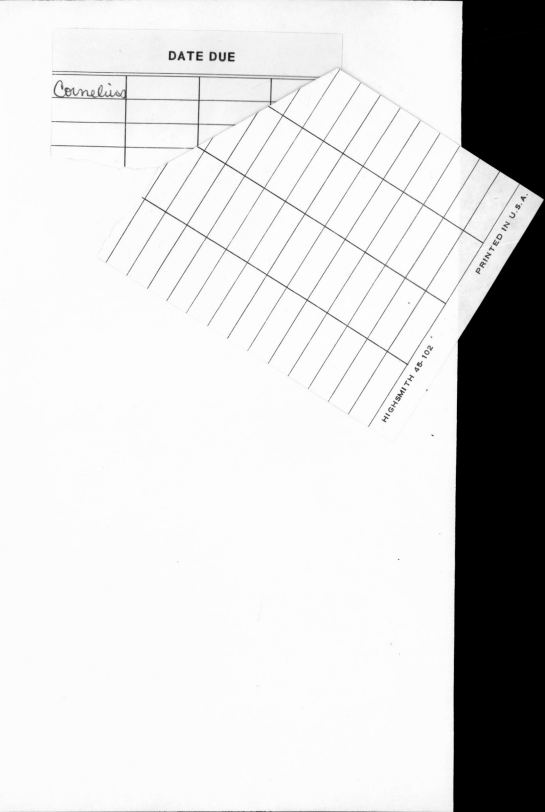

DATE DUE

Cornelius

HIGHSMITH 45-102

PRINTED IN U.S.A.